IRA PECK

Cover Photo: George C. Scott as General George S. Patton, Jr.
in the Frank McCarthy-Franklin J. Schaffner production PATTON,
based on factual material from *Patton: Ordeal and Triumph* by
Ladislav Farago and *A Soldier's Story* by Omar N. Bradley, a 20th
Century Fox release.

SBS SCHOLASTIC BOOK SERVICES
New York Toronto London Auckland Sydney

Photo Credits

United Press International: Pages 6, 19, 24, 46, 57, 60, 63, 68, 75, 125, 128, 130, 131, 134, 135. Brown Brothers: Pages 5, 22, 28, 41, 48, 49, 84, 85, 94, 102. Wide World: Pages 11, 14, 35, 44, 74, 83, 100, 137, 143. Culver Pictures: Pages 64, 65, 72, 106, 110, 116, 117, 119, 120. Army News Features: Pages 27, 78, 80. Signal Corps Photo: Page 103. Acme Photo: Page 40.

Grateful acknowledgment is made to Holt, Rinehart and Winston, Inc. for permission to reprint the maps used herein from A SOLDIER'S STORY by Omar N. Bradley. Maps by Rafael Palacios. Copyright 1951 by Holt, Rinehart and Winston, Inc.

1st printing......................December 1970
Printed in the U.S.A.

CONTENTS

Gen. George S. Patton displays his "war face" during World War II.

CHAPTER I: ✰ ✰ ✰ ✰
THE ANATOMY OF A HERO

The face was set in an almost ferocious scowl. The chin thrust forward aggressively against a taut helmet strap. The corners of the mouth turned down, and a hard glint shone from narrowed eyes.

This is the way that most Americans—those who are old enough—remember General George S. Patton, Jr., one of this country's most spectacular and successful World War II army commanders. Patton called this hard-as-nails look his "war face." It was not a look that had come to him naturally. By his own admission, he had practiced it in front of a mirror throughout his life. Patton considered play-acting an important part of being a military commander. In fact, he was almost as adroit a showman as he was a battle tactician.

Consider, for example, his uniform. From head to toes, everything was spit-and-polish. His helmet gleamed brilliantly, the result of dozens of coats of varnish that were applied to it. His jacket fit him perfectly, and was immaculate. The stars designating his rank, as well as the brass buttons, sparkled; rows of campaign ribbons gave a bright splash of color. Around his waist was a broad leather belt, and at his hips was a pair of ivory-handled pistols that were his trade mark. His riding breeches and his expensive leather boots were nothing less than elegant. Standing tall and erect, chest out, shoulders back, he was an imposing figure.

Patton's showmanship was not just a matter of appearance, however. He was a master of the art of profanity and prided himself on being able to "cuss out" a man for two or three minutes at a time without having to repeat a single swear word. His "pep talks" to his troops were

"Spit-and-polish" was the mark of Patton's uniform. He is shown here with Generals Eisenhower, Bradley, and Hodges (left to right).

laced with the rawest of language and sometimes embarrassed even battle-hardened veterans. A very mild example of his profanity in these talks, most of which are unprintable, is this statement made to his men shortly before the invasion of Sicily:

"Now, I want you to remember that no son-of-a-bitch ever won a war by dying for his country. He won it by making the other poor dumb son-of-a-bitch die for *his* country."

Patton liked to use words for their shock effect, even when they were not necessarily profane. "Rip your bayonets into the bloody bowels of the enemy," he would tell his men. "Rip 'em up the belly, or shoot 'em in the guts!"

Patton's flair for cursing helped him attain his reputation as a tough soldier and commander. There were some men who served with Patton who boasted of having been "cussed out by the old man." It was almost a badge of honor. To others, it must have been very painful, for Patton could be quite savage when he wanted to be. Once, for example, a long column of guns, vehicles, and troops was stalled on a road in France. The lead vehicle, a half-track mounting a 155 mm. gun, was jammed under a low concrete bridge. The column would have been a sitting duck for German artillery had it been spotted by enemy reconnaissance planes.

Patton, who was driving along this road, sized up the situation and became furious. Approaching the officer in charge of the column he snapped, "Colonel, you can blow up the goddam gun, you can blow up the goddam bridge, or you can blow out your goddam brains — I don't care which you do."

All these things — the angry scowl, the arrogant bearing, the pistols at his hips, the brutal exhortations to spill blood, the cursing and the butt-kicking — had a definite

7

purpose. They were intended to create the impression that General George S. Patton, Jr., was the roughest, toughest, meanest soldier in this man's army.

It was a pose that fooled many people, but not the more perceptive ones. It certainly didn't fool Patton's boss, General Dwight D. Eisenhower, Supreme Commander of the Allied forces in Europe. In his book, *Crusade in Europe*, Eisenhower assesses Patton in these words:

"Many men who believed they knew him [Patton] well never penetrated past the shell of showmanship in which he constantly and carefully clothed himself. . . . All the mannerisms and idiosyncracies he developed were of his own deliberate adoption. One of his poses, for example, was that of the most hard-boiled individual in the Army. Actually, he was so softhearted . . . that it was possibly his greatest fault."

One can cite numerous instances of Patton's softheartedness. On one occasion, for example, Patton was riding in an open command car near Colmar, France, in freezing weather. Noticing that his driver was shivering, Patton asked the man if he was wearing a warm sweater. When the driver replied, "No, sir," Patton peeled off his own and gave it to him. Eisenhower cited another example. One day Patton demanded that Ike discharge 80 of his (Patton's) officers for being incompetent and timid — almost cowardly, in fact. Ike rather astonished Patton by agreeing to do it just as soon as Patton sent him a list of the men's names. For weeks Patton kept putting it off. Finally, when confronted by Ike, Patton sheepishly confessed that he didn't want to discharge anyone.

Patton undoubtedly was softhearted. If he was quickly moved to anger, he was almost as easily moved to tears. Almost any sentimental gesture — a display of loyalty or affection on the part of his staff, for example—would bring tears to his eyes. Yet Patton's he-man pose could have been a cover-up for feelings that ran much deeper than mere softheartedness or sentimentality. Patton's nephew, Fred Ayer, Jr., suggests it was used to cover up "the inner conflict that tormented him . . . the contrast between [his] belief . . . that battle was romantic and chivalrous and brave, and the realization that it was dirty, gut-wrenching, and very dreadful. . . ." In his adoring biography of Patton, *Before the Colors Fade*, Ayer describes the following scene, which took place two nights before Patton was to sail for the invasion of North Africa's shore:

"It was after dinner in [our] living room in Wenham, Massachusetts. Patton became overdramatic, almost hysterical . . . in his conversation. There were tears in his eyes. 'It's awful,' he said. 'It's terrible, that's what it is. I can see it in a vision. It comes to haunt me at night. I am standing there knee-deep in the water and all around as far as the eye can see are dead men, floating like a school of dynamited fish. And they're all floating face up with their eyes wide open and their skins a ghastly white. And they're all looking at me as they float by and saying, "Patton, it's your fault. You did this to me. You killed me." I can't stand it, I tell you. By God, I won't go. I won't go.' "

Patton did go, of course, and did his job unflinchingly. But clearly his job *did* cause him a great deal of torment. It is difficult to reconcile this image of Patton with the more familiar image of the man who once said, "Compared to war, all other forms of human endeavor shrink to insignificance. God, how I love it!"

Just before the invasion of Sicily, Patton had this to say to his troops:

"Battle is the most magnificent competition in which a human being can indulge. It brings out all that is best; it removes all that is base. All men are afraid in battle. The coward is the one who lets his fear overcome his sense of duty. Duty is the essence of manhood. Americans pride themselves on being he-men, and they *are* he-men."

Here was Patton talking about manhood, fear, and cowardice. On this occasion, at least, Patton made a reasonable distinction between fear and cowardice. Yet, all too often, Patton tended to equate them. As a consequence, evidence of fear in other men thoroughly appalled him. Even more, he was appalled by the idea of ever showing fear himself. Patton was constantly sticking his neck out on the battlefield to prove to himself that *he was not afraid*, a fact that did not go unnoticed by his colleagues. A few years ago, General James M. Gavin wrote:

"We occasionally speculated about why George made such a spectacle of himself with his glossed helmet, ivory-handled pistols, and stars wherever he could place them on his uniform. We wondered why he felt that he should urinate off the first pontoon bridge over the Rhine River, or make forays not too far from enemy fire. A close mutual friend told me that George had assured him that he [Patton] was more afraid of showing fear than anything else, and that since he knew fear often in battle, he behaved in this manner to cover up his true feelings."

This, then, was the basic contradiction in Patton: a man who reveled in war, yet felt a great sense of guilt about having to send men to their death; a man for whom war brought out everything that was manly, yet feared that he himself might not measure up; a man who talked and acted tough because he sensed, as others did, that he was really quite softhearted.

Patton watches his tanks roll through El Guettar valley in Tunisia. One of his ivory-handled revolvers can be seen at his right hip.

This was the greatest contradiction in Patton's makeup, yet it was by no means the only one. Despite all his coarseness and vulgarity, Patton was a well-educated, civilized man who could recite from memory long portions of the *Iliad*, Shakespeare, the Bible, and the poems of Rudyard Kipling. He even wrote poetry himself, though it was not very good and was obviously inspired by Kipling. He had an almost encyclopedic knowledge of history, particularly military history, and could remark quite casually that a certain road being travelled by his tanks in France was the same one used by some Roman legions about 2000 years ago. He was probably right, too.

Despite his profanity, Patton was a religious man — at least by his own lights — who knelt in prayer before every battle and invoked the blessings of the Deity. Apparently, he saw no contradiction at all between his coarseness and his feelings of religious devotion. On one occasion, an Army chaplain visiting Patton's headquarters in France saw a copy of the Bible on his desk. Patton had been on his best behavior during the clergyman's visit, but he reacted strongly when the chaplain asked him if he really read the Bible. "Goddammit," Patton replied, "I read it every day!"

Though Patton used raw language in addressing his troops, he was in other respects a quite puritanical man. He was usually almost absurdly chivalrous towards women, and he resented anything that he thought debased them. Once a battallion under his command in the United States gave a stag party and invited Patton to be the guest of honor. When an almost nude dancer came on stage to perform, Patton became furious and walked out. The next morning his subordinates received a blistering memorandum from Patton on how officers and gentlemen were expected to behave.

There was at least one other major contradiction in Patton's character. Though as a combat commander he was a shrewd, tough-minded realist, otherwise he was possessed of a very strong streak of mysticism. He believed, for example, that he had been reincarnated many times, and that he had fought on many different battlefields throughout history. He expressed this belief in one of his poems, "Through a Glass Darkly":

> So as through a glass and darkly
> The age-long strife I see
> Where I fought in many guises,
> Many names—but always me.

> And I see not in my blindness
> What the objects were I wrought
> But as God rules o'er our bickerings
> It was through His will I fought.

So forever in the future,
Shall I battle as of yore
Dying to be born a fighter,
But to die again once more.

Once in North Africa during World War II, British General Sir Harold Alexander pleased Patton by remarking, "You know, George, you would have been a great marshal for Napoleon if you had lived in the 18th century." Patton smiled and said, "But I did."

Patton believed, too, that he possessed extrasensory powers, including telepathy and clairvoyance. But above all else, he believed in a sense of *destiny*, and he had no doubt about his own. "All my life I have wanted to lead a lot of men in a desperate battle," he wrote on the eve of the invasion of North Africa. "Now I am going to do it." To become a great battlefield commander—that was the destiny that Patton always believed would be his. How well he succeeded is, of course, a matter of history. But consider the opinions of two of Patton's contemporaries, General Eisenhower and Field Marshal Karl von Runstedt, Commander-in-Chief of the German armies in the West during the momentous Battle of the Bulge:

At the end of World War II, Ike said: "No one but Patton could exert such an extraordinary and ruthless driving power at critical moments or demonstrate the ability of getting the utmost out of soldiers in offensive operations."

Von Runstedt put it with Prussian terseness when he told a reporter after Germany's surrender, "Patton—he was your best."

Patton looked both proud and stern as cadet at Virginia Military Institute. Later he switched to U.S. Military Academy at West Point.

CHAPTER II: ✩ ✩ ✩ ✩
THE MAKING OF A WARRIOR

Had George S. Patton, Jr., become anything but a soldier, it would have been truly remarkable. Everything in his background and upbringing made his choice of soldiering as a career almost inevitable. Everything in his background, too, made it inevitable that he would pursue it as an officer and a gentleman.

Patton came from an old and highly respected Virginia family. His great-grandfather, John Mercer Patton, had been an esteemed lawyer, a Congressman, and, briefly, Governor of Virginia. John Patton had eight sons, six of whom fought for the Confederacy in the Civil War. (The two who didn't were too young to bear arms at the time.) One of them, Col. George Smith Patton, was killed in action near Winchester, Virginia, in 1862, when he was 26. This man was General Patton's grandfather and namesake, and an idol whom he always sought to emulate. Col. Patton's widow, left with two sons and a daughter, but hardly a penny, married one of her husband's friends, Col. George Hugh Smith. A dashing cavalry officer, Smith found the defeat of the Confederacy more than he could bear. After the war, he moved to California to start a new life as a lawyer.

His stepson, George S. Patton II, attended Virginia Military Institute and was graduated at the top of his class. Instead of a military career, however, he chose to practice law in his stepfather's office. In time he became quite successful and was elected District Attorney of Los Angeles County. A handsome young man, he married the daughter of a California rancher who had accumulated enormous holdings in the San Gabriel Valley. George Patton II and his wife settled down to married life on an 1800-acre ranch cut out of his father-in-law's vast estate.

Their son, christened George S. Patton, Jr., although really the third Patton to bear the name, was born on November 11, 1885. His was a happy, tranquil, and affluent home. As a youngster, "Georgie" had everything that a boy could want, including ponies, guns, fishing tackle, and boats.

The atmosphere around the Pattons' ranch home had decidedly military overtones. Grandfather Smith talked endlessly about the glories of Confederate arms in the Civil War, and invited old cronies to the home. One of them was Col. John Mosby, a cavalry officer who served under "Jeb" Stuart and later carried out slashing guerrilla raids against Union forces. It was not unusual for Mosby to conduct mock Civil War battles in which Georgie would pose as General Robert E. Lee. In addition, George's father frequently took him to visit old Civil War battlefields where they reenacted the fighting.

George's father was an intelligent, cultured man, but he did not believe much in formal education for his children. Rather than send George to school where he would be crammed with the three R's, he undertook to educate the boy himself. He read the classics to his son, with emphasis on Homer, the Bible, and Shakespeare. As a result, George could recite long passages from them by memory, but until he was almost 12 he could neither read nor write. That situation was finally remedied when George was enrolled in a private school in Pasadena in his 12th year.

Whether or not George's father actually wanted him to become a soldier, he could not have done a better job of instilling in him such an ambition. To young George, raised on tales of Confederate derring-do and ancient Greeks besieging the walls of Troy, war must have seemed incomparably romantic, exciting, and adventurous — "The most magnificent competition in which a human being can engage." From the time he was a boy and ran around with a wooden sword, George never wanted to be anything else but a great general. At an early age, he was already concerned with the problem of becoming tenderhearted in battle and conditioning himself against such a dread possibility. On one occasion, for example, he forced himself to eat an orange while gazing steadily at a dead frog well along in decay.

George was graduated from Pasadena High School, and in the fall of 1903 entered Virginia Military Institute, the school that both his father and grandfather had attended. At the end of a year, having absorbed some of the tradition of his forebears, George switched to the U.S. Military Academy at West Point, New York. Unfortunately, in his "plebe" (freshman) year, George flunked math, which made it necessary for him to start all over the following fall.

At West Point, George played football with more zeal than skill, suffering two broken arms and fracturing his nose three times. He did better in track, winning his letter in that sport by bettering an Academy record in an outdoor meet. As a student, George excelled in "Drill Regulations," and in his senior year was made Corps Adjutant, a post awarded to the cadet with the best record for military bearing and discipline. George was not the most popular young man in the Corps, as it was often his job to impose discipline on other cadets. His boast that he would be the first man in his class to become a general (he wasn't) didn't sit well with his classmates, either. In his class yearbook there is this rather barbed comment about him:

"It is said that Georgie Patton has compiled for future generals a rule for winning any battle under any combination of circumstances."

George was graduated from West Point in 1909, standing 46th in a class of 103. In the meantime, the Corps disciplinarian had not been impervious to a well-placed arrow from the bow of Cupid. In the summer of 1902,

17

George had met 15-year-old Beatrice Ayer, a Boston girl who was visiting relatives on Catalina Island, where the Pattons also had a cottage. Bea was rather small for her age, but she was a good rider, swimmer, and sailor and well able to keep up with George. Before the summer was over, the two had reached an understanding that neither would date any other. They wrote to each other regularly, and after George entered West Point he began courting Bea in earnest.

Bea's father, Frederick Ayer, was a wealthy and aristocratic New England industrialist who maintained palatial homes in Boston and on Cape Cod. Although the Pattons were wealthy and aristocratic in their own right, Ayer was not pleased at the prospect of having a soldier for his son-in-law. Neither did he relish the prospect of his daughter living in rough-and-tumble Army outposts. When George asked Ayer for his daughter's hand in marriage, Ayer asked George to write him a letter explaining why he had chosen the Army for a career. This is what George wrote:

"With reference to the profession of a soldier, I think I appreciate most of its drawbacks. As you say, it is very narrowing, but don't you think that a man of only very ordinary capacity, in order to succeed against great competition, must be narrow? I have no experience, but from what I read of successful men, they seem to be the one-idea sort.

"It is hard to answer intelligently the question: 'Why do I want to be a soldier?' For my own satisfaction, I have tried to give myself reasons, but have never found any logical ones. I only feel it inside. It is as natural for me to be a soldier as it is to breathe and would be as hard to give up all thought of it as it would be to stop breathing.

"But being a soldier and being a member of the Army

18

Lt. Patton in 1910, when he was with cavalry at Fort Sheridan, Ill.

in time of peace are two different things. I would only accept the latter as a means to the former."

Apparently the letter had its effect, for Ayer consented to the marriage. The wedding, a very social affair, took place near Salem Harbor, Massachusetts, almost a year after George's graduation from West Point. After a honeymoon in England, Second Lieutenant George Patton took his bride to his first Army post, Fort Sheridan, Illinois. There Patton was attached to Troop K, 15th Cavalry Regiment.

If Frederick Ayer had misgivings about his daughter living on Army posts, Bea soon found out why. In 1910, Army life was anything but glamorous. The nation was at peace, no major power threatened it, and Congress saw little reason to lavish large appropriations on the armed forces. The pay of both officers and enlisted men was pitifully small and advancements extremely slow.

It might take 15 years for a man to be promoted from second to first lieutenant. The living quarters for officers and their wives were less than luxurious. At Fort Sheridan, Patton and his wife occupied two tiny rooms in a small house on the post, hardly the style of living to which either was accustomed.

Nevertheless, the Pattons decided to make the best of it. George and his wife dressed for dinner every night, and he drove around in the fastest car that money could buy. Later, whenever possible, the Pattons rented fairly splendid homes in smart residential areas and George sped to his posts in high-powered cars. This high style of living did not make the Pattons popular with other officers and wives who had to live on meager Army salaries.

If there was any branch of the service that was glamorous in those days, it was probably the cavalry. It permitted Patton, as part of his regular duties, to participate in such exclusive sports as polo, cross-country riding, fox-hunting, and horse shows. Wherever the Pattons went, they were part of the "horsey set," and their names frequently appeared in newspaper society and sports columns. Patton, in fact, maintained his own stable of polo ponies and other horses, and took them with him from one post to another. His arrival at a new post was usually something of an event, which did not always endear him to his commanding officers. Once, in 1915, Patton's C.O. threatened to have him court-martialed if he didn't get his horses off the post promptly. Patton arranged to have them stabled nearby at his own expense.

Being independently wealthy had other advantages, as well as the obvious disadvantages, for Patton in the peacetime Army. In 1912, the Olympic games featured a "modern pentathlon" event in which military athletes were to compete. This pentathlon had competitions in fencing, pistol-shooting, horseback riding, cross-country running, and swimming. The event appealed to Patton, and at his own expense he travelled to Stockholm, Sweden, to take part in it. Always a tough competitor, Patton pushed himself hard to prepare for the games. On the voyage to Sweden, for example, he practiced swimming by tugging against a rope in a wooden tank built on the ship's deck.

In Stockholm, Patton put on quite a show. He twice knocked himself out trying to win. He took first place in fencing; he finished third in the 300-meter swim and had to be pulled out of the pool with a boat hook when he passed out at the end; he finished third in riding; and he finished third in the cross-country race, passing out again from sheer exhaustion at the finish line. The only competition in which Patton did poorly was pistol-shooting, and this was probably the result of a fluke. All but one of his shots hit the bull's-eye, but one could not be accounted for at all. The judges ruled that Patton had missed the target completely with that shot, but it is more likely that it had gone cleanly through a previous hole. Because of the judges' ruling, Patton finished only 27th in the pistol-shooting, but wound up in fourth place for the overall competition, a quite respectable showing.

In 1916, Patton reached the summit of his early Army career. That year, a Mexican bandit leader named Pancho Villa raided a border town in New Mexico, and the shoot-out took 16 American lives. President Wilson immediately ordered General John J. Pershing to lead a "pu-

Gen. John J. Pershing leading U.S. cavalry in Mexico, 1916.

nitive expedition" into Mexico to capture the bandit chieftain. Here was a chance for some real, live action, and Lt. Patton had no intention of missing it. For two days, he camped at General Pershing's door. Every time Pershing appeared, Patton begged him to take him on the expedition. After several refusals, Pershing finally relented and took Patton along as his aide and as a scout.

Neither Patton nor any other member of the 10,000-man "punitive expedition" saw very much action in Mexico. Villa was an elusive foe, and almost invariably he and his *banditos* kept one step ahead of the pursuing Americans. The expedition was finally recalled without having accomplished its mission. Yet Patton did take part in one shoot-out that would have done credit to any Western movie. One day, Pershing ordered Patton to visit a few Mexican *haciendas* (large farms) and buy corn for the American troops. Patton took some enlisted men with him and set out in a couple of touring cars. At one hacienda, Patton had a hunch that Villa's chief bodyguard, Julio Cardenas, and other bandits were hiding out. He was right. There was a short but decisive gun battle in which three of the bandits, including Cardenas, were killed. Patton himself accounted for two of them with his ivory-handled pistol.

Patton then strapped the bodies of the two men he had killed onto the fenders of his car and drove back to Pershing's headquarters. Pershing, who was normally a taciturn man, was impressed. "That Patton boy!" he said, *"he's a real fighter."* Pershing promoted Patton to first lieutenant. The following year, when the United States was drawn into World War I, Pershing was named commander of the American forces in France. Pershing chose Patton to be his junior aide and commandant of his headquarters.

Lt. Col. Patton stands smartly beside a World War I tank.

CHAPTER III: ✰ ✰ ✰ ✰
PATTON IN WORLD WAR I

Patton arrived with General Pershing in France in June 1917, and began organizing training facilities for the large numbers of U. S. troops that would follow. At first Patton found his job exciting, but soon it began to pall on him. For a man whose ambition was to become a great combat commander, administrative work had definite shortcomings. In September, Patton told Pershing about his discontent, and Pershing offered him a choice of either commanding an infantry brigade or taking an assignment in the "American Tank Corps." The choice proved something of a dilemma to Patton. The infantry did not intrigue him; it was, he felt, a rather dull, colorless service. In spirit, Patton was a cavalryman, longing for fast, slashing action. Cavalry, however, was already an anachronism in World War I, principally because of the development of machine guns and other advanced weapons.

What about tanks? These had been developed by both the British and the French to break the stalemate of trench warfare in World War I. But so far they had proved exceedingly unreliable in combat. They suffered from frequent mechanical failures and were prone to bog down in mud and over rough terrain. Even more depressing to Patton was the fact that the American Tank Corps then existed only on paper. In 1917, the U.S. Army had just one crude, experimental tank. It would have to employ British or French tanks for its new corps. On the basis of the tanks' past performance, such a prospect could hardly have inspired Patton with enthusiasm.

To resolve his dilemma, Patton wrote to his father-in-law, Frederick Ayer, for advice. Ayer's answer was as follows:

"I know nothing of war. But my advice to you would be to choose the weapon with which you believe you can inflict the most punishment on the enemy while at the same time suffering the fewest casualties yourself."

Ayer's letter enabled Patton to make a decision. He promptly informed Pershing that it was his wish to be assigned to the Tank Corps, and Pershing granted it. The Tank Corps now consisted of two men, its commander, Brigadier General Samuel D. Rockenbach, and his Chief of Staff, Captain George S. Patton, Jr. Patton's job was to train and command two battalions of tanks which would form the First Brigade of the new U. S. Army Tank Corps.

25

Patton knew nothing about tanks and had to school himself at British and French training centers. Once he had mastered the technique of operating a tank, Patton recommended that the embryonic Tank Corps adopt the small, light French Renault model. Weighing only six tons and operated by a two-man crew, the Renault was more mobile than the 30-ton monsters the British were using, and Patton chose it for this reason. Even so, it was a very primitive vehicle. Its top speed was five miles an hour, and often it could not keep up with the infantry that it was supposed to precede. Inside the Renault, the driver sat on the floor while the gunner stood in the turret. The gunner gave the driver directional signals by kicking him on the head or shoulders — that was the only way they could communicate. Like all tanks in those days, the Renault was prone to break down, and usually at least half of them were laid up for repairs at any given time.

The first group of 22 Renault tanks for the American Tank Corps arrived one night at a railroad siding near Langres, where Patton had set up his training center. (He was, by this time, a lieutenant colonel.) Aroused from his sleep, Patton spent the next few hours driving the tanks off the railroad flat cars. He had to — so far he was the only one at Langres who knew how to operate a tank. The Tank Corps, however, was attracting a number of volunteers and Patton swiftly began the job of training his brigade and getting it into fighting shape. Patton was a tough disciplinarian and drove his men hard. He was already beginning to gain a reputation as "the worst martinet in the U.S. Army." Patton was not disturbed by this. Basically he believed that strict training and discipline made men better soldiers and, as a

Yanks go "over the top" with bayonets fixed in World War I.

consequence, saved lives. Patton used to sum it up very succinctly by saying, "A pint of sweat saves a gallon of blood." And while Patton's men may have grumbled and muttered under their breaths, they also took pride in their reputation for proficiency and smartness. A real snappy salute in this outfit was known as "a George Patton."

By the summer of 1918, Patton had whipped his tank brigade into shape. Patton, however, was becoming anxious. His chief worry was that the war might end before he and his tank brigade ever got into action. So far, the Americans generally had seen little action in France. Late in July, however, plans were drawn up for a major American offensive in the St. Mihiel area, and Patton's tanks were assigned an important role. The attack was set for September 12.

At 1 A.M. on that day, the artillery began its preliminary

barrage. Four hours later, the infantry was to go "over the top." Patton's tanks were to precede the foot soldiers and give them cover until they reached the German lines. For a while it almost appeared that Patton's tanks would not get into action after all. The trains on which they were being transported were late, and some of the Renaults did not reach Patton until well after the artillery barrage had started. Patton fumed and swore, but by 3:15 A.M. all his tanks were on the line and ready to go into action.

When the order to advance was given at 5 A.M., Patton was standing on a hill from which he could watch his tanks as they moved ahead. What he saw was, in his own words, "a most irritating sight." It had been raining hard in the area, and soon one tank after another began to bog

Patton's tanks move up to the battle line in World War I action.

down in the mud. Those that did not get stuck in the mud got stuck in the German trenches, some of which were eight feet deep and 10 to 14 feet wide. Of the 174 tanks that started forward at 5 A.M., only 70 were still operating by daylight.

Patton dashed all over the battlefield that morning in an effort to keep his remaining tanks in action. (World War I tanks carried no radio equipment. Tank commanders had to lead their vehicles on foot.) Patton ran from tank to tank with pistol in hand, urging them forward. There was plenty of German artillery fire, and Patton saw one of his tanks blasted by a shell moments after he had left it.

With some of his tanks, Patton moved on to the town of Essey. There he assisted in its capture by infantrymen commanded by Brigadier General Douglas MacArthur. Patton and MacArthur chatted briefly, but, according to Patton, "neither was much interested in what the other said as we could not get our minds off the shells."

Patton and his tanks then proceeded towards the town of Pannes. All except one of the tanks ran out of gas along the way, but Patton ordered the one remaining tank into Pannes anyway. To reassure the nervous crewmen, Patton sat on top of the vehicle as it rode into town. Moments later, Patton heard the clatter of machine-gun bullets and saw the paint flying off the side of the tank. Instantly Patton leaped off and threw himself into a shell hole. Unaware that Patton had jumped off, the tank kept moving ahead. Fearful for the tank's crewmen, if not his own life, Patton left his shell hole and, dodging machine-gun fire, ran to get infantry support. The infantry, however, was not yet ready to advance, so Patton had to race back to the tank to tell it to withdraw. Just at that moment, four more of his tanks entered the town with infantry and the Germans pulled out.

Patton then walked to the town of Nonsard where he found the 25 tanks that had captured it completely out of gas. Although thoroughly exhausted by this time, Patton headed back on foot to an airfield where he ordered aviation gasoline sent up to his stalled tanks. Then he jumped on a motorcycle and rode back to his headquarters to report to General Rockenbach on the day's activities.

If Patton expected to be complimented by Rockenbach for his heroics, he could not have been more wrong. Rockenbach, in fact, gave him a severe dressing down. He accused Patton of trying to win the war single-handedly and of exposing himself unnecessarily to enemy fire. He threatened to relieve Patton of his command until Patton apologized and promised to behave himself in the future.

In a letter to his wife, Bea, describing the day's action, Patton wrote:

"I at least proved to my own satisfaction that I have nerve. I was the only officer above the rank of major on the front line except General MacArthur who never ducked a shell. . . . General Rockenbach gave me hell for going up, but it had to be done. At least I will not sit in a dugout and have my men out in the fighting."

Despite his promise to General Rockenbach to behave more discreetly in the future, Patton set out the very next morning on an unauthorized mission. He ordered a large number of his tanks to advance toward the Hindenburg Line, a series of fortifications to which the Germans had retreated from St. Mihiel. So far, U.S. infantry had not yet moved up to the Line, leaving a void, or "no man's land," between the Germans and the Yanks. On Patton's orders, three of his tanks actually penetrated the Hindenburg Line and engaged in battle with a German artillery battery, which they knocked out. The three tanks then withdrew, but Patton was so elated with his success that he elected to remain in "no man's land" for some time. German artillery was beginning to get the range on his tanks when Patton received a message from General Rockenbach. Alerted to Patton's foray, Rockenbach ordered him to cut short his private war with the Germans and report to him immediately.

If Rockenbach had been angry with Patton the day before, he was furious with him now. Once again Patton solemnly and abjectly assured his commander that he would give him no more trouble in the future and somehow got off the hook. But Rockenbach thought it expedient, nevertheless, to write to Mrs. Patton about her husband. He implored her to exercise some restraint on Patton, as he apparently could not.

The St. Mihiel offensive accomplished its objectives in just two days, somewhat to Patton's chagrin. But now a vast new offensive was being planned for the Americans in the Argonne-Meuse sector, which the Germans had heavily fortified since 1914. More than 1,200,000 Yanks were assigned to drive the Germans out of this wooded, hilly area, and once again Patton's tank brigade was to take part. On September 25, Patton was alerted for the attack which was to begin the next day at 4:25 A.M. after a three-hour artillery barrage.

The guns were lined up almost hub to hub for miles, and their rapid-fire bombardment of the German lines that morning was shattering. The Germans, however, were well dug in and their resistance was staunch. As at St. Mihiel, Patton's tanks—135 in all—failed to make much of an impression despite Patton's own best efforts. German artillery took a heavy toll of them, as did the difficult terrain and numerous mechanical failures. Once again Patton dashed around everywhere on foot, trying desperately to keep his remaining tanks moving forward.

It was almost inevitable that Patton would be hit by enemy fire, and in fact it happened that very day. While escorting five of his tanks through a hole in the German lines, Patton came across some 300 infantrymen who were pinned down by heavy German machine-gun fire. Wishing to exploit the breakthrough, Patton summoned the doughboys to follow him through the hole. The doughboys, however, were more impressed with the German fire than they were with Patton's bravado and elected to stay put. Finally Patton called for volunteers. Five men, including his orderly, Sgt. Joe Angelo, offered to follow him. It was a suicidal mission, and within minutes three of the men had been killed and a fourth wounded. Only Sgt. Angelo was still following behind Patton. Thirty yards from the secondary German trenches, Patton was struck by a machine-gun bullet that ripped a large hole in his upper thigh and sent him reeling into a shell crater.

Sgt. Angelo jumped in after him and did his best to stem the flow of blood from Patton's wound. Though

Patton was in shock when the medics arrived, he insisted on being taken to a division headquarters to make his report rather than being evacuated to a hospital. Patton passed out while making his report and consequently could not protest when he was finally removed to a hospital behind the lines.

In later years, Patton told his nephew, Fred Ayer, Jr., just what made him charge the German machine guns:

"I was lying on my belly and scared to death, hardly daring to lift my head. But finally I did and looked up to a bank of clouds glowing reddish in the almost setting sun. And then, just as clear as can be, I saw their heads, the heads of my Virginia grandfather and his brothers . . . I could read their eyes, and they said to me, 'Georgie, you're a disappointment to us lying down there. Just remember, lots of Pattons have been killed, but there never was one who was a coward.' So I got up, drew my gun, and gave commands. And at the last, Col. George and the others were still there, but smiling."

From the hospital, Patton wrote to his wife that he was "missing half my bottom" but otherwise was all right. As might be expected, Patton was a restless patient. The news that the Germans were slowly being pushed back and that the war might end any day filled him with despair. When he could bear it no longer, Patton managed to obtain a car and with a friend deserted the hospital. He got back to the front on November 11, 1918, his 33rd birthday, only to hear the "bad" news: The Germans had signed an armistice agreement and the war was over.

Patton was to suffer one other disappointment at this

time. He fully believed that he would be awarded the Distinguished Service Cross for his brief, one-day part in the Argonne offensive. He was deeply upset when he learned he was *not* going to get it. The next day Patton wrote to his wife:

"The most terrible thing has happened to me. I heard last night I will not get the D.S.C. I woke up all last night feeling that I was dying, and then it would occur to me what had happened. I cannot realize it yet. It was the whole war to me, all I can ever get out of two years away from you. But I will be goddamned if I am beat yet. I do not know what I will do, but I will do something."

Patton suspected, perhaps rightly, that General Rockenbach had something to do with his not getting the D.S.C. Rockenbach, in fact, had been quite incensed about Patton's "unauthorized leave" of the hospital and was threatening Patton with punishment. Patton managed to avoid it by appealing in person to General Pershing. Pershing was completely won over by his protégé and forgave him his indiscretion.

Patton now began a campaign to win the D.S.C., badgering people close to Pershing and influential in the War Department. Finally, on January 1, 1919, Pershing himself presented the coveted medal to Patton. The citation accompanying the medal praised Patton for "conspicuous courage, coolness, energy, and intelligence in directing the advance of his brigade" and later rallying "a force of disorganized infantry and leading it forward behind the tanks under heavy machine-gun and artillery fire until he was wounded."

Patton holds blue ribbon won in 1929 horse show.

CHAPTER IV:
PATTON BETWEEN WARS

If the end of World War I came as a blow to Patton, the events that followed were almost as hard to take. In a wave of revulsion against the blood-letting of World War I, disarmament became the order of the day. In the U.S., Congress again pared military appropriations to the bone, and the Army was reduced to an inconspicuous force. When the war ended, Patton was a full colonel in command of a brigade in the Tank Corps. The Corps had won a niche for itself in the Army, in large measure because of Patton's own efforts, and Patton was allowed to retain his command. Thereafter, however, Patton's fortunes began to decline rapidly as disarmament took hold.

Soon after his return to the United States in May 1919, Patton was reduced in rank to major and his tank brigade became little more than a curiosity. Appropriations for the Tank Corps were so meager that Patton had only enough gas to run his vehicles a few minutes a day at Fort Meade, Maryland. Patton, however, was not prepared to take the virtual demise of the Tank Corps lying down. He was by this time an ardent proponent of tanks, and he attempted several experiments to improve them, sometimes at his own expense. His main hopes lay with a New Jersey mechanic and racing driver named Walter Christie. In 1919, Christie was developing a revolutionary new tank capable of cruising at 30 miles an hour.

Patton arranged a demonstration of the Christie tank one day at Fort Meade with several generals in attendance. The demonstration tank was a primitive affair, little more than a platform mounted on wheels. Nevertheless, Patton praised its virtues to the visiting brass. It was not only much faster than World War I tanks, Patton said, but it was so easy to handle that a child could drive it. He invited his guests to try it, but all politely declined. Patton then turned to his wife and said, "All right, Bea, *you* demonstrate it." Thoroughly unruffled, Mrs. Patton, in her street clothes, did demonstrate the tank quite skillfully. The generals, however, were merely embarrassed. Eventually the Army turned down the Christie tank. (Later it would become a mainstay of the Soviet Union's Red Army.)

In 1920, when Congress allotted just 500 dollars to the Army for tanks, Patton saw the handwriting on the wall and rejoined his old service, the cavalry. Now, in an effort to accommodate himself to the spirit of the times, he championed the cause of cavalry in various articles for Army publications and downgraded tanks, the most expensive weapons in the Army's arsenal.

It was difficult, at best, for Patton to be diplomatic. By nature he was outspoken and contentious. He could, on occasion, charm people, but he really preferred to shock them. At dull social gatherings, for example, he was apt to approach some hapless society matron, open his belt buckle, and offer to show her where he had been wounded in World War I. At a party given in honor of some young British Army officers, he made a speech in which he asserted that Britain, not Germany, was responsible for the outbreak of war in 1914.

Ultimately, Patton was no more diplomatic in his relations with the Army. His high style of living continued to antagonize senior officers, while his insistence on keeping his men in a state of instant readiness for war both baffled and irritated them. At a time when the nation *and* the Army were peace-minded, Patton's mounting advocacy of full military preparedness rankled high Army officers. In 1928, when Patton was serving in Hawaii, he received a severe rebuke from his commanding officer, Major General William R. Smith. Smith summoned Patton to his office and personally read to him portions of the efficiency report he had just written on Patton. It concluded with this comment:

"This officer would be invaluable in time of war, but is a disturbing element in time of peace."

Patton put the best face on it by thanking General Smith for his "great compliment."

Patton was again severely rebuked by a commanding officer in 1936 when he was serving a second tour of duty in Hawaii. As usual, Patton sought relief from the tedium of peacetime service by engaging fiercely in rugged equestrian sports. One day, the Army polo team captained by Patton was playing a championship match against a civilian team made up of society sportsmen. The stands were full of spectators, men and women, and in the very first row was Major General Hugh A. Drum, the Army's commanding officer in Hawaii. During the match, Drum became increasingly irritated with Patton's swearing, which could be heard "loud and clear" in the stands. (Patton had a high-pitched voice which became shrill when he got angry.)

Finally Patton collided with a player on the civilian team and let loose some really choice invectives. This was too much for General Drum. At the end of the period, he ordered Patton off the field "for using offensive language in front of ladies and insulting your competitors." Patton was quite stunned, but moments later members of the civilian team interceded. They told Drum that they would cancel the match unless Patton was allowed to resume playing. Drum was furious, but there was little he could do except restore Patton to the Army team. He never forgave Patton, and he, too, gave him an extremely poor efficiency report. The two men remained bitter enemies.

Patton's career was very much on the skids. He was now 50 years old and, after 27 years in the Army, was still only a lieutenant colonel. Patton began to think about retiring and bought a handsome estate near Boston for that purpose. Then he suffered a near-fatal accident, the result of being kicked by a horse. For days he was in critical condition, threatened by a blood clot that was travelling towards his heart, but finally he pulled through. Convinced that his luck had not yet run out on him, Patton elected to have another go at the Army.

This is how Patton described the experience to his nephew, Fred Ayer, Jr.:

"I know that I passed out, and then was aware that I was lying on some battlefield on a big Norse shield. After a while, two armored Vikings came and started to lift me up on that shield to carry me to Valhalla. Then one of them shook his head, and they gently put me down again, and I came to in my bed. I guess they're not ready to take me yet. I still have a job to do."

For a time, Patton's luck did seem to improve. But then, on July 1, 1938, he was assigned to a quiet old cavalry post at Fort Clark, Texas, where over-aged officers were usually sent as a prelude to retirement. Though promoted to a full colonel at the time, Patton was on the way out.

He was saved from oblivion by events that were taking place a long way from the Texas panhandle post, where once the cavalry had ridden out against the Indians. In January 1933, Adolf Hitler, leader of the Nazi party in Germany, took power in that country. His goal was nothing less than world conquest. Ignoring the Versailles Treaty, which limited Germany's armed forces after World War I, Hitler built a powerful war machine and embarked on a course of aggrandizement. After annexing Austria and dismembering Czechoslovakia, he began to menace Poland. Meanwhile, Hitler's allies, Italy and Japan, were also dismembering or swallowing weaker nations.

Though far removed from the United States, these

Gen. George C. Marshall plucked Patton from obscurity in 1938.

events did not go unnoticed in this country. One of those who saw the gathering war clouds in Europe was General George C. Marshall, who, in October 1938, became Deputy Chief of Staff of the U.S. Army. (Soon after, he was promoted to Chief of Staff.) Marshall believed that a second world war was imminent, and that sooner or later the United States would be drawn into it. He had also observed the revolutionary concepts of warfare that were shaping the new German Army — mechanization, mobility, and speed. Influenced by such men as Heinz Guderian and Erwin Rommel, the Germans were pinning their hopes on swift, armored *panzer* units in which tanks were the principal weapon.

Marshall soon began drawing up a list of names of men whom he felt could cope with the demands of future warfare. One of the names on his list was George S. Patton, Jr. Marshall, who had helped plan the St. Mihiel and Argonne offensives in World War I, remembered Patton as the man who had trained the Army's

German armored forces swiftly overran France in May-June, 1940.

first tank brigade and led it so aggressively in combat. In November 1938, Marshall ordered Patton transferred to Fort Myer, Virginia, in order to have him near Washington, D.C.

At first, Patton's life did not change substantially. He instituted his usual spit-and-polish regime at Fort Myer, and kept up the usual fast round of partying and horse shows. Not even the outbreak of World War II on September 1, 1939, when Germany invaded and then swiftly conquered Poland, changed things much. The war in Europe still seemed quite remote. Then, in May 1940, Germany's mechanized armies launched a "blitzkrieg" (lightning war) attack against France and the Low Countries. By June 20, Germany had conquered western Europe. Now the Nazis were masters of most of the continent.

Marshall began strengthening the U.S. Army in every way that he could. On July 10, he created an Armored Force with two divisions, as an attempt to meet the challenge of German mechanization. He appointed George Patton to command a brigade of the 2nd Armored Division, to be formed at Fort Benning, Georgia. Within a few weeks, Patton was promoted to the rank of brigadier general.

Despite his new prestige, Patton was anything but happy with the situation he found at Fort Benning. His tanks were antiques that were ready for the scrap heap. (It would be some time before the Army's new Sherman tanks would start coming off the assembly lines.) He kept them going by ordering makeshift spare parts from Sears, Roebuck, usually paying for them out of his own pocket. Then another problem developed. The troops that began filling up his command in the fall of 1940 were mostly draftees, men who had been plucked from civilian life by their draft boards only weeks before. Unlike the doughboys of 1917, they had little enthusiasm for Army life, and even less for the kind of strict discipline imposed by Patton.

In an effort to instill in them some of his own warrior spirit, Patton began delivering the first of his fire-eating speeches to his troops. Sgt. Joe Rosevich, who was Patton's secretary throughout most of the war, never forgot the first time Patton dictated one of them to him. Patton, he said, dictated the speech quite calmly. Then, after Rosevich had typed it up, Patton rehearsed it in front of him. According to Rosevich, Patton worked himself into a furious state while reading the obscenity-strewn oration. When Patton had finished, he sat down and quite calmly explained the whole business to his astonished secretary. This is the way Rosevich tells the story in *Patton, Ordeal and Triumph*, by Ladislav Farago:

"Patton said that the performance I had just watched was just that—a performance, a put-up show, a calculated and rehearsed act of bravado. He was convinced, he said, that the young men of America needed such a toughening because they had grown soft and careless. . . .

"Patton said with emphasis: 'You cannot change the mental habits of these boys overnight. You have to shock them out of their ordinary habits and thinking with the kind of language you've just heard in the speech. . . . It's a boisterous method of training and commanding men. But it's certain to pay dividends in ground gained and lives saved!'"

It was at this time, too, that Patton acquired the nickname that stuck with him throughout the war—"Blood and Guts." In a rousing speech to a group of officers, Patton said that an armored division needed "blood and brains" to be effective in combat. Newspaper reporters got wind of the speech, but somehow garbled it. They said that Patton had called for "blood and guts." The phrase caught on and eventually Patton was tagged with it.

Patton's flair for showmanship was already reaching a high point at Fort Benning. Deciding that his tankers needed a distinctive uniform to set them apart from ordinary soldiers, Patton designed one and wore it himself. It was distinctive, all right. It was green with black stripes down the sides of the pants and buttons that ran diagonally across the jacket. It was topped off with large goggles and a gold helmet that Patton had obtained from the Green Bay Packers football team. The first time Patton wore it, one of his tankers exclaimed, "Look—the

Patton models his Green Hornet outfit at Fort Benning, Georgia.

Green Hornet." (The Green Hornet was a popular comic strip character of the day, somewhat like Batman.) Patton could not get the Army to adopt the uniform for his men, but Patton wore it anyway. Soon generals were visiting Fort Benning on almost any pretext, but really to see Patton in his Green Hornet get-up.

A few weeks after his arrival at Fort Benning, Patton was promoted to major general and given command of the 2nd Armored Division. Patton drove his men relentlessly, putting them through back-breaking maneuvers. "War is a killing business," he admonished them. "You've got to spill their blood or they'll spill yours." Although the men griped under the pressure, they soon came to pay their commander a kind of begrudging respect. "You better don't lay an egg before the Old Man," they would tell a newcomer. "He doesn't like it."

In the summer of 1941, the U.S. Army was scheduled to begin the biggest and most realistic war games in its history. The 2nd Armored Division would have its first real test in massive maneuvers to take place in Tennessee. For Patton, there was more at stake than a mere exercise in make-believe combat. Army brass at this time was still sharply divided over the value of armored forces in warfare, despite the overwhelming success of the German panzers in Europe. Many were convinced that tanks were overrated, and that good antitank weapons would stop them cold. Patton, of course, was an ardent advocate of tank warfare and had read everything that Guderian and Rommel had written about it. Like the Germans, Patton saw the main function of tanks as breaking through the enemy lines and then spreading havoc from the rear. (This was a far cry from their role in World War I, which was simply to escort infantry up to the enemy trenches.) Patton summed up his philosophy of battle this way:

"Battles are won by frightening the enemy. Fear is induced by inflicting death and wounds on him. Death and wounds are produced by fire. Fire from the rear is more deadly and three times more effective than fire from the front. But to get fire behind the enemy, you must hold him by frontal fire and move rapidly around his flank. Frontal attacks against prepared positions should be avoided, if possible."

Patton often summed up this philosophy in one earthy sentence:

"Catch the enemy by the nose and then kick him in the pants."

Patton was determined to prove his theories of mobile, armored warfare in the Tennessee maneuvers. He was doubly eager to prove them because he suspected, perhaps rightly, that the rules regulating the war games had been rigged in favor of the antitank theoreticians.

Patton's tanks jumped off on June 20, 1941, and soon they were running wild, making a shambles of the carefully prepared exercise. Striking out on wide end runs, they captured "enemy" command posts so swiftly that General Leslie J. McNair, who was in charge of the exercise, had to call it off 12 hours ahead of schedule. Patton had taken so many objectives there was nothing left to do.

The next maneuvers involving the 2nd Armored Division were scheduled for September 15 in Louisiana and east Texas. This time General McNair was determined that Patton's tanks would not run wild again. He told his umpires before the games:

"These exercises are designed to test tank warfare in the face of intelligent antitank defenses. We are definitely out to see if and how we can crush a modern tank offensive."

The Louisiana-Texas maneuvers, however, were the same story. The 2nd Armored Division slashed out in

Gen. Patton drives one of his tanks during training maneuvers.

all directions, capturing command posts, cutting communications, and generally disrupting the orderly conduct of the exercises. To top it off, Patton led the 2nd Armored on a spectacular 380-mile sweep through eastern Texas and "captured" Shreveport, Louisiana, from the rear. This time McNair had to call off the maneuvers a day in advance, and he was furious.

The last maneuvers of the year were to take place in the Carolinas in November. This time, there was some added spice to the games for Patton. The commander of the forces his 2nd Armored Division would oppose was none other than his old adversary, General Hugh A. Drum. Drum's army was equipped with substantial antitank units designed to stop Patton in his tracks. This was more of a temptation than Patton could resist, even if he had wanted to. Less than one hour after the 2nd Armored had jumped off on November 16, General McNair received the following message at his headquarters:

"Lt. General Drum captured in Chester, South Carolina, by elements of the 2nd Armored Division."

In his report on the maneuvers, General McNair sharply censured Patton, charging him with "too many piecemeal attacks" and adding that this was "no way to fight a war."

Patton, however, was jubilant. On returning to Fort Benning with his men, he issued an order complimenting them on their fine performance in the maneuvers. The order was dated December 6, 1941. The next day, Japanese planes bombed Pearl Harbor, Hawaii, and the United States was at war. Now Patton would have a chance to fight against real enemies and to realize his life-long ambition of becoming a great combat commander.

U.S. troops under Patton's command go ashore at French Morocco, near Casablanca.

CHAPTER V: ☆☆☆☆
WORLD WAR II:
PATTON IN NORTH AFRICA

Soon after the attack on Pearl Harbor, Patton was given a new assignment. He was ordered to set up and command a training center for armored forces in the area of the Great American Desert. Patton chose a site near Indio, California, after inspecting it from the air in his private plane and later driving through it. The Indio Desert Training Center covered a vast area, about 180 miles long and 90 miles wide, and was thoroughly awful: Temperatures daily reached 120 degrees, there was no shade, and violent dust storms were a constant menace.

While Patton was toughening up his men at Indio for

future combat, the question of when and where U.S. troops would actually engage German forces was being debated elsewhere. Among the American planners, particularly General Marshall, there was strong sentiment for an invasion of western Europe across the English Channel as early as 1942. Among the planners of our British allies, however, there was no enthusiasm at all for such a scheme. Because of America's lack of preparedness at the time, the brunt of an invasion in 1942 would have had to be borne by the British, and they knew that they did not have the resources to carry it out. For although the bulk of Hitler's armies, about 165 divisions, were then tied up in a vast invasion of Russia, some 63 divisions, still a formidable force, had been left in western Europe to oppose any Allied invasion attempt.

Finally the American and British planners agreed on a compromise scheme. This would be an invasion of North Africa in the fall of 1942 to oppose the Axis pow-

Gen. Erwin Rommel, head of Germany's Afrika Corps, won reputation as "the desert fox." Patton wanted to fight him.

ers—Germany and Italy—there. This would relieve
General Sir Bernard Montgomery's British Eighth Army,
which was then retreating before General Rommel's
Afrika Corps in Libya, and, it was hoped, take some
pressure off the beleaguered Russians.

The plan for the invasion of North Africa, which was
given the code name "Torch," called for three separate
landings. Two of them would be made inside the Mediterranean at Oran and Algiers. These coastal cities were
part of Algeria, which was then a French colony. The
third landing would be made on the Atlantic coast near
the city of Casablanca, French Morocco, which was then
a French "protectorate." On July 30, 1942, General
Marshall summoned Patton to Washington and offered
him the job of commanding the invasion of French
Morocco. After seeing the plans, Patton dismayed ev-

**Invasion plan for North Africa called for landings at three points.
Patton's Western Task Force was to take Casablanca.**

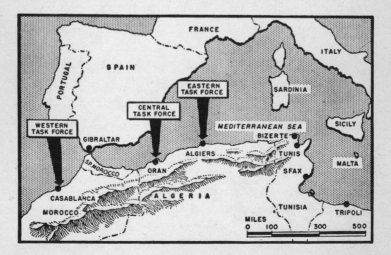

eryone by declining it. Patton's reason was that the number of troops and ships allotted to him were not enough to accomplish the mission. Marshall grimly sent Patton back to Indio. There were no more troops or ships to spare.

Three days after his return to Indio, Patton had a change of heart. On August 2, he was on the phone, pleading with Marshall's deputy for the job. The next day he was back in Washington to begin work on his phase of Operation Torch. Patton soon found that his own misgivings about Torch were widely shared by other members of the American and British high command. German submarine "wolf packs" were a serious menace to Allied ship convoys at this time, and there was a dearth of warships to protect an operation as large as Torch. In addition, landing craft were still in short supply, and on the Atlantic coast, where Patton had to land, the tides were extremely treacherous. Oddly enough, the more pessimism that Patton encountered, the more enthusiastic he himself became about Torch. On one occasion he remarked, "This may not be the best show, but it's much better than nothing. I am determined to see it through."

By the middle of October, Patton's Western Task Force was set to leave from Norfolk, Virginia. Now Patton began making his farewells. He paid a sentimental visit to his old commander, General Pershing, at Walter Reed Hospital and described the scene in his diary:

"He [Pershing] did not recognize me until I spoke. Then his mind seemed quite clear. He looks very old. It is probably the last time I shall see him, but he may outlive me. [Pershing did.] I said that when he took me to Mexico in 1916, he gave me my start. He replied, 'I can always pick a fighting man and God knows there are few of them. I am happy they are sending you to the front at once. I like generals so bold that they are dangerous. . . .'

"When I left, I kissed his hand and asked for his blessing. He squeezed my hand and said, 'Good-bye, George, God bless you and keep you, and give you victory.' I put on my hat and saluted. He returned it like he used to, and 25 years seemed to drop from him. . . ."

Patton also bade farewell to his Commander-in-Chief, President Franklin D. Roosevelt, at the White House. At the end of their meeting, Patton told FDR, "Sir, I will leave the beach either a conqueror or a corpse." Later that day, he repeated the line as he said good-bye to General Marshall.

On October 24, 1942, Patton's Western Task Force set out from Norfolk to begin the two-week voyage to French Morocco. (Two other task forces, due to land at Oran and Algiers, left from British ports the next day.) As it reached the open sea, the convoy was an imposing sight. As far as the eye could see, columns of gray ships were moving in perfect formation across the ocean. The convoy was comprised of 36 transports, cargo vessels, and tankers, escorted by 68 warships, including three battleships and five aircraft carriers. They covered an area 30 miles long and 20 miles wide. On board the cruiser *Augusta*, Patton wrote in his diary, "It seems that my whole life has been pointed to this moment."

Outwardly confident, inwardly Patton fretted a good deal about his mission while at sea. He frequently bolstered his confidence by repeating a motto that he borrowed from an idol, General "Stonewall" Jackson: "Do not take counsel of your fears." Three unknown factors were troubling Patton as the convoy steamed across the Atlantic:

1. French Morocco, like Algeria, was part of the French empire in North Africa. It was ruled by representatives of the Vichy government in France. This government, headed by Marshl Henri Pétain, was committed to a policy of collaboration with Nazi Germany. What would be the attitude of the Vichy representatives in North Africa towards the Allied invasion? Would they resist it forcefully or merely make a show of token resistance? In French Morocco they controlled more than 60,000 troops as well as strong naval forces. Patton had fewer than 34,000 troops under his command. If the French were to put up strong opposition, then Patton's early pessimism about his prospects might well have been justified.

2. What would the Germans do? Would Hitler send his armies into neutral Spain, take over Gibraltar, and then move across the narrow straits into adjacent Spanish Morocco? If so, Patton's chances of success would be very dim.

3. What kind of surf conditions would the Western Task Force encounter on the beaches of French Morocco? Normally the beaches were swept by waves 15 feet high, enough to capsize any landing vessel. On about 12 days a year, the beaches were relatively calm. Patton would be very lucky indeed to arrive during one of these brief lulls.

As the convoy stealthily zig-zagged its way across the Atlantic, the threat of German submarines did not materialize. But three days from French Morocco, on November 5, the convoy ran into a severe storm that did not bode well for the impending landing operation. At 2 A.M. on the morning of November 8, Patton could see the lights of Casablanca from the flag deck of the *Augusta*. Almost miraculously, the sky had become clear and the sea dead calm. "God is with us," Patton noted in his diary.

Patton's plans called for three separate landings in the vicinity of Casablanca. One would take place at Fedala, immediately adjacent to the city. A second would take place at Safi, to the south, and a third at Port Lyautey, to the north. Although the arrival of the Western Task Force took the Vichy French commanders by surprise (and the Germans, too), any hopes that they would surrender without a fight were quickly dashed. Soon after the first predawn landings at Fedala, French shore batteries and warships began firing on the task force. When daylight came, a hot naval battle developed, and Patton had to remain aboard the *Augusta*. By noon, the French fleet, including the battleship *Jean Bart*, had been virtually destroyed, and Patton was finally able to start ashore.

As Patton's crash boat neared the beach, he spotted an ammunition landing craft that was stuck on a sand bar. Jumping over the side of his boat, Patton waded over to the stalled craft and took charge of the struggle to free it. Putting his own shoulder to the task, Patton exhorted the men to "Push, godammit, push! How in hell do you expect to win a war without ammunition?" Soon the landing craft was freed and Patton began setting up his headquarters on the beach.

The landing at Safi, Patton learned, was going smoothly, with few casualties. But at Port Lyautey, the story was different. There native Moroccan troops and French Legionnaires were fiercely defending an ancient *kasbah*, or fortress. Bloody hand-to-hand fighting took place before the Americans finally subdued it with the aid of bazookas and self-propelled artillery.

Immediately upon his arrival at Fedala, Patton had sent a messenger to Admiral Francois Michelier, chief of the French naval forces at Casablanca, in an effort to persuade him to surrender· peacefully. Michelier had not only refused, he had furtively alerted other French forces to resist the American landing. Now, hoping to avoid further bloodshed, Patton sent another messenger to Michelier, who again stubbornly refused to surrender. Throughout the next day, Patton's forces made only small gains against the French garrison defending Casablanca; Patton was still hoping that Michelier would come to his senses and accept the inevitable. Then, on November 10, Patton received a telegram from General Eisenhower, who was supervising the entire North African operation from his headquarters at Gibraltar. The telegram said:

"Dear Georgie: Algiers has been ours for two days. Oran defenses are crumbling rapidly. . . . Only tough nut left to crack is in your hands. Crack it open quickly. Ike."

Stung by Eisenhower's telegram, Patton swiftly ordered an all-out attack on Casablanca for the next morning. That night, however, Michelier received a message from his superior in Algiers, Admiral Jean Darlan, ordering him to surrender. Michelier delayed carrying out the order for several hours, and meanwhile Patton refused to cancel his attack. At 6:48 A.M., only minutes before U.S. ships and planes were set to begin bombarding Casablanca, Patton received word that the French had officially capitulated. Only then did he call off the assault. "Thank God," Patton said as he heard of the French surrender. To his wife, Bea, he wrote: "Those hours were the longest in my life so far."

Now, only 73 hours after the initial landings at Fedala, Patton was the master of French Morocco. His next job was to negotiate a peace agreement with the top French officers there, Admiral Michelier, General Auguste Nogues, and others. Patton had been supplied with two peace treaties by the U.S. State Department. One, whose terms were lenient, was to be used by Patton if the French surrendered without a fight. The other, whose terms were much harder, was to be used by Patton if the French resisted, which they had. Patton read to the French officers the terms of the "hard" treaty. Michelier declared it, in a word, "unacceptable." General Nogues protested that it would virtually strip the French of their power in Morocco, and warned Patton that it would result in chaos and disorder.

At that point, Patton rose, tore up the treaty, and made a brief speech. He said, in effect, that they were all officers and gentlemen and could therefore trust each other. He had known some of them since World War I, when they had been allies. All he wanted was their solemn assurance as gentlemen that they would no longer bear arms against his forces, and that they would maintain order and discipline within the country. The French, of course, were delighted with the terms of Patton's "gentlemen's agreement" which kept them in power, and a clink of champagne glasses sealed the bargain.

Patton's assumption that men like Michelier and Nogues could be trusted proved unfortunate. While he was being feasted and treated to magnificent displays of military pageantry by the Sultan of Morocco, Nogues was quietly jailing all those French officers

Patton shakes hands with Sultan of Morocco following surrender of French. French General Auguste Nogues stands behind them.

who had tried to aid the American invasion. Nogues also kept in force the Nazi racial laws discriminating against Jews and permitted pro-German propaganda broadcasts to continue over the Moroccan radio. In 1947, Nogues was sentenced *in absentia* by a French court to 20 years at hard labor as a Nazi collaborator.

Although Patton did obtain the release of some French officers jailed by Nogues, the situation was bad enough to infuriate pro-Allied Frenchmen and move Prime Minister Winston Churchill to write a letter of protest to President Roosevelt. (The honeymoon with Vichy representatives in North Africa generally was soon terminated and later the Allies recognized the "Free French" forces of General Charles DeGaulle as the legitimate French representatives.)

During this time, Eisenhower was moving rapidly eastward towards Tunisia with Allied forces that had landed in Algeria. Tunisia was the main supply base for the German Afrika Corps, and Ike was hoping for a swift knockout blow there. Once they had recovered from the surprise of the Allied landings in North Africa, however, the Germans managed to build up their forces in Tunisia considerably. By December, the Allied advance was stopped cold by a combination of stubborn German resistance and heavy winter rains that turned the battlefield to mud.

Then, in February 1943, the Germans launched a counterattack in Tunisia. At Kasserine Pass, panzer units led by General Rommel mauled elements of the U.S. II Corps before withdrawing. As a consequence, morale and discipline in the II Corps began to suffer. Soon Eisenhower was looking for a new commander to take over the II Corps and revive it as an effective fighting force. The man he chose was Patton. In his book, *Crusade in Europe,* Ike wrote: "Morale in the II Corps was shaken and the troops had to be picked up quickly. For such a job, Patton had no superior in the Army."

On the morning of March 7, Patton arrived at the headquarters of the II Corps in Tunisia. He was riding in the lead car of a procession of armored scout vehicles and half-tracks, with sirens screeching and machine guns bristling. According to General Omar Bradley who was on the scene, "Patton stood like a charioteer. He was scowling into the wind and his jaw strained against the web strap of a two-starred steel helmet."

Almost immediately, Patton began a series of disciplinary measures designed to shock the II Corps out of its lethargy. All troops, including mechanics, were required to wear helmets, leggings, and neckties at all times. A system of fines ranging up to $25 for enlisted men and $50 for officers was instituted to enforce the regulation. Patton himself sought out offenders, and he did not overlook the latrines in his diligence. At the same time, Patton prohibited the officers' mess from serving breakfast after 6:30 A.M. By the third day, Patton had the II Corps fighting mad—but at Patton, rather than the Germans. Bradley, who was in Tunisia as Ike's personal representative, made this comment in his book, A Soldier's Story:

"I could not accustom myself to the vulgarity with which Patton skinned offenders for relatively minor infractions in discipline. Patton believed that profanity was the most convincing medium of communication with his troops. But while some chuckled delightedly over the famed expletives he employed with startling originality, the majority, it seemed to me, were more often shocked and offended. At times I felt that Patton, however successful he was as a commander, had not yet learned to command himself.

"The techniques of command vary, of course, with the personality of the commander. While some men prefer to lead by suggestion and example and other methods, Patton chose to drive his subordinates by bombast and by threats. Those mannerisms achieved spectacular results, but they were not calculated to win affection among his officers or men."

In little more than a week, when the II Corps was again scheduled to go into action, Patton had left no doubt that he was boss. And, whether or not they liked their new boss, the men of the II Corps had undoubtedly shaped up. Meanwhile, Patton had taken another significant step. Though he did not dislike Bradley personally, he believed that Bradley had been sent by Eisenhower to snoop on him. "I'm not going to have any goddam spies running around my headquarters," he growled. Then he resolved the problem neatly by calling Eisenhower's headquarters and requesting that Bradley be made deputy commander of the II Corps. If this were done, Bradley would become Patton's subordinate. Ike was happy to comply. He had Bradley in mind for an even more important role later on.

By the middle of March 1943, the German and Italian forces in Tunisia were beginning to buckle. They were caught in a huge pincer movement: While British and U.S. forces were pushing in from the west, Montgomery's British Eighth Army was pushing up from the southeast. (In October 1942, Montgomery had inflicted a major defeat on the Afrika Corps at El Alamein in Egypt. In a span of 80 days, he rolled Rommel's vaunted

British troops chase Germans after El Alamein victory.

Corps back 1,750 miles to Tunisia.) Allied strategy at this time called for Montgomery to make an all-out attack on his front to crack the Germans' Mareth Line defenses. Patton and the II Corps were assigned to make a diversionary attack in the area of Gafsa and El Guettar, northwest of the Mareth Line. The night before the attack on Gafsa, set for March 17, Patton met with his staff for a final briefing. "Gentlemen," he concluded, "tomorrow we attack. If we are not victorious, let no one come back alive." Then, while his staff was still stunned by his rhetoric, Patton retired to his room to pray.

The attack on Gafsa turned out to be little more than a walk-in, and El Guettar fell swiftly, too. But beyond El Guettar, German resistance stiffened. On March 23, the Germans struck back with panzer units in a frantic effort to shake Patton off. (Rommel, whom Patton had always wanted to meet in combat, did not command the attack. A sick man, he had given up his command in Africa and returned to Germany.) At 6 A.M., just as the sun was rising, about 50 German Mark II and Mark IV tanks rolled across a valley floor towards Patton's lines. They were supported by infantry and outdated Stuka dive-bombers. Though forward elements managed to penetrate the American positions, by 9 A.M. the attack was halted. Then the Americans were tipped off by radio intercepts that the Germans would renew their attack at 4:40 that afternoon. This time the II Corps was waiting for them. As the German tanks and infantry advanced, Patton's artillery held its fire until they were in easy range. Then the guns blasted the attackers with concentrated fire. As the German forces wavered, Patton remarked, "They're murdering good infantry. What a hell of a way to waste good infantry troops."

Finally the German attackers halted and then with-

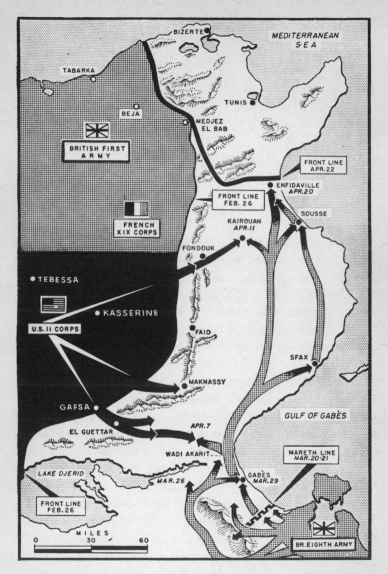

While the British Eighth Army under Montgomery attacked Mareth Line, the U.S. II Corps under Patton struck toward El Guettar.

Patton watches the II Corps battle the enemy near El Guettar.

drew. Thirty-two of their tanks were left behind in flames. Patton had done his job well, applying pressure that helped Montgomery break through the Mareth Line. Yet Patton was disappointed by his limited role in the fighting. He believed he could have done a great deal more, but he was under orders not to proceed much beyond El Guettar. This was the first time, but by no means the last, that Patton would feel that he was being shackled by the Allied high command, which he considered to be dominated by the British. It would be a consistent complaint of his as the war progressed. In any event, Patton did not mind it very much when, on April 5, Eisenhower turned over the II Corps to Bradley for the balance of the Tunisian campaign and reassigned Patton to Morocco. Patton was to resume planning the next big phase of the Allied operation against Germany and Italy—the invasion of Sicily. As for the Tunisian campaign, it ended on May 20, with Allied prisoner-of-war camps bulging with sullen Germans and happy Italians. In such fashion did Operation Torch go into history.

Patton wades ashore in Sicily, a cameraman in front, a soldier holding a carbine behind him. He was often near enemy fire.

CHAPTER VI: ★★★★
PATTON IN SICILY

In January 1943, President Roosevelt, Prime Minister Churchill, and the top Allied military leaders met at Casablanca, where General Patton was their host. The purpose of the Casablanca conference was to determine future Allied strategy. What would be the next step against Germany and Italy once their forces had been defeated in North Africa? Once again, the British were most reluctant to attempt an invasion of Europe across the English Channel. Churchill advocated instead a series of campaigns against the enemy in the Mediterranean area, which he called "the soft underbelly of Europe." General Marshall believed that such a policy was shilly-shallying, and would never bring Germany to its knees. Marshall argued that only a cross-Channel invasion would ultimately defeat Germany. Yet the fact was that the North African campaign had already diverted so many of the Allies' resources to the Mediterranean area that a cross-Channel invasion in 1943, with limited forces, would have been extremely hazardous. Finally, a compromise was agreed upon: Marshall acceded to an invasion of Sicily in 1943 in return for a definite British commitment to a cross-Channel invasion in 1944.

What were the advantages that an invasion of Sicily might offer? For one, Axis aircraft based on Sicily were a menace to Allied shipping in the Mediterranean. Once the island was wrested from the Axis, that menace would be eliminated and the same airfields could then be used to launch Allied raids on the continent. Another advantage was that an invasion would maintain the momentum of the Allied offensive against the Axis; the alternative might have been an idle summer in North Africa. Finally,

Invasion of Sicily was agreed upon by President Roosevelt, Prime Minister Churchill, after much debate at Casablanca conference.

it would help keep Russia in the war by engaging enemy strength that might otherwise be used against the Red Army on the eastern front.

Patton had begun planning the invasion of Sicily, which was given the code name "Husky," in February 1943. He was temporarily diverted from the task when Ike summoned him to take command of the II Corps in Tunisia. Now, in April, Patton was back at work on Husky. Husky was to be a combined U.S. and British operation. Patton would lead the U.S. Seventh Army, which was then in the process of being assembled. General Montgomery, the hero of El Alamein, would lead the British Eighth Army. Both would serve under the group command of General Sir Harold Alexander, a widely respected British officer. Once again, Eisenhower would be the Supreme Commander.

Invasion plan for Sicily called for British to land near Syracuse, U.S. Seventh Army in Gela area. Final goal was port of Messina.

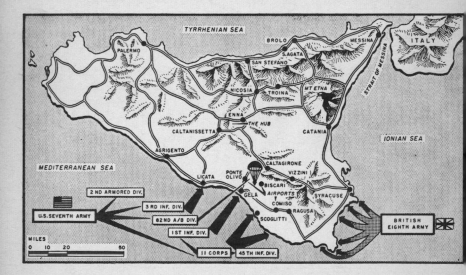

The Allies' principal objective in Sicily was the port of Messina in the northeast corner of the triangular island. This port lies very close to the Italian mainland, and it would be the natural escape route for the Germans once they had been defeated in Sicily. Patton favored a two-pronged attack on Messina. In this plan, Montgomery's army would land near Syracuse at the southeast corner of the island and then proceed directly north to Messina. Patton's army would land near Palermo at the northwest corner of the island and then advance eastward towards Messina. Montgomery, however, took exception to this plan. Expecting fierce Axis opposition, he strongly questioned the wisdom of dividing the two Allied armies. Instead, Monty proposed that the two armies land close together in the southeast corner of the island. His army would land near Syracuse on the right. Patton's army would land on a wide strip of beaches on either side of Gela to the left.

Basically, this was the plan that the Allies finally adopted. It thoroughly infuriated Patton. He would be landing on an extended area of beaches exposed to enemy counterattacks, with only one small port, Gela, to supply him. Montgomery would be landing on a much narrower front, and would have a major port to supply him—Syracuse. Even more objectionable from Patton's point of view, Monty would eventually have the glory of taking Messina. For in this plan, while Monty moved directly up the east coast towards Messina, Patton's army would move up on his left through central and western Sicily, nowhere near Messina. Patton's function basically would be to protect Montgomery's flank, and there was little glory in that for Patton. He would again be playing second fiddle to Montgomery, and he did not relish the role.

Montgomery, center, and Patton, right, study map of Sicily, where their rivalry heated up. It was sometimes friendly, often bitter.

Patton was not only angry with Montgomery, he was angry with Eisenhower as well, for Ike had given his approval to this plan. To Patton this was a betrayal, and evidence, he felt, of "Allyism" or a pro-British bias on Ike's part. Patton's developing rivalry with Montgomery would persist throughout the war, and Ike would have the unenviable task of having to choose between their often conflicting demands.

The invasion of Sicily was set for the predawn hours of July 10, 1943. On July 5, the U.S. convoys set out from three widely separated North African ports, and then converged as they approached Sicily. At one minute past midnight on July 10, Patton made a brief speech to a group of high-ranking officers aboard the command ship *Monrovia*. "Gentlemen," he said, "I have the honor and privilege to activate the United States Seventh Army. This is the first army to be activated after midnight and baptized in blood before daylight." Then Patton was presented by an honor guard with a gift for his brand new army of 80,000 men—the stars and stripes. The ceremony brought tears to Patton's eyes. To one observer, "Patton stood not upon a ship's deck, but upon a peak of glory."

At 2:45 A.M., the first U.S. forces began going ashore. They met with very little opposition. The Germans had assigned only third-rate Italian forces to the defense of the beaches, and these quickly surrendered or beat a hasty retreat. The main threat to the American invaders lay behind the beaches where the Germans were holding their armored forces in reserve until they could be sure of the landing locales. To the rear of the American beachhead at Gela, the crack Hermann Goering panzer division was waiting to hurl the GI's back into the sea.

The German counterattack came on the morning of July 11, one day after the Seventh Army had begun landing. At 6:40 A.M., Brigadier General Kermit Roosevelt of the 1st Division reported that panzers had broken through on his front near Gela and were headed toward the beach. "We're going to have a helluva time stopping them," he told his C.O., Major General Terry Allen, "unless we get some antitank stuff ashore."

The 1st Division's artillery and antitank guns were still being unloaded from landing craft. Meanwhile, the lightly armed infantry units were being overrun by German tanks. Two columns of Mark IV's, about 60 in all, were converging on the beach at Gela in an attempt to break through to the water's edge. If they succeeded, the entire beachhead would be endangered.

Now Allen ordered every gun in his division rolled into position to meet the tanks at point-blank range. Trucks raced from the beach with additional artillery pieces as they came off the landing craft. From offshore, warships also began to shell the Germans. Though they were overrun, the soldiers of the 1st Division did not break. Instead, they dug into foxholes and let the tanks roll through. Then they waited for the German infantry following behind the tanks. With the help of the naval artillery support, they held the line. The German counterattack was stopped outside Gela, and more than 30 Mark IV's were destroyed. The Germans attacked again in the afternoon, but this time heavy fire from U.S. Navy cruisers sent them scurrying for the hills. Now the beaches were secure.

Meanwhile, Patton had shown his customary bravado, dashing around the front in a jeep and exposing himself to enemy fire on several occasions. At one point, shells were exploding only 30 yards from where he was standing on the beach. Later he drove six miles along a road *between* the American and German lines, which he himself noted in his diary was "quite unusual for an Army Commander." Finally, Patton saw "the most stupid thing I have ever seen soldiers do." A few GI's were digging foxholes between stacks of bombs and shells that had been unloaded onto the beach. Patton told them that that was a fine thing to do *if* they wanted to save the Graves Registration people trouble. Otherwise he urged them to dig their foxholes elsewhere. Just then two British Hurricanes came over to strafe the beach, and the men jumped into their holes. In his diary, Patton wrote, "I continued to walk up and down and shamed them into getting up. . . . This is the first day in this campaign that I think I earned my pay."

In a letter to his wife soon after, Patton described an incident in which he came under German shell fire:

"I was disgusted to find that my pulse went up—I timed it—but soon I got myself in hand. I can have a shell hit or a mine go off quite close without winking or ducking. This is a great asset . . . one must be an actor. Besides, if they are going to get you, they hit you before you hear them."

After consolidating their beachheads in southeast Sicily, Patton's Seventh Army and Montgomery's Eighth Army began pushing north as planned. Within a few days, however, Monty's forces were bogged down before Catania on the east coast. Here Montgomery had run into a bottleneck. On his right was the sea, and on his left was the great volcano, Mount Etna. Before him were German panzer units blocking his path. To break the stalemate, Monty would have to bypass Mount Etna on the western side. But in the meantime, Patton had gone to General Alexander on July 17 to propose that the Seventh Army be allowed to share in the capture of Messina. By now Alexander realized that Montgomery was not strong enough to take Messina by himself, and he gave Patton a green light. The Seventh Army was to drive north, split the island in two, and then push east to Messina. Now Patton directed units of his army to capture Palermo, the city that he had wanted to take originally. In a lightning thrust that covered 100 miles in four days they entered Palermo on July 22. The rapidity of the advance stunned the Italian government, and, three days later, Benito Mussolini, the Fascist dictator, was toppled from power.

Soon Patton was pushing towards Messina. By the end of July, however, his forces were stopped outside the hilltop town of Troina, where the enemy had built a very strong defensive line. For three days their attacks were thrown back by savage resistance from crack German panzer and grenadier units. "Troina's going to be

Patton points with a swagger stick on Sicily invasion beach.

tougher than we thought," General Terry Allen reported. "The Kraut's touchy as hell here."

For the first time in the war, the fighting was going badly for Patton and he was visibly upset. It was at this time that he became involved in two incidents with hospitalized soldiers that almost ended his career. On August 3, discouraged by the news at Troina, Patton visited a field hospital in General Bradley's II Corps sector. Patton chatted with the wounded men, tried to cheer them up, and told them he was grateful to them. Then, as he was leaving, Patton saw one soldier who had no visible wound. Patton asked the young GI what was wrong with him.

"I guess I just can't take it," the soldier replied.

In fact, the soldier was suffering from a nervous condition brought on by the stress of combat. (In World War II, the condition was generally called "combat fatigue.") For Patton, to whom combat was the acid test of manhood, such a man was not ill; he was simply a coward. Patton lost control of himself. He slapped the young soldier with his gloves, kicked him, and called him "gutless." Then he ordered the hospital C.O. to return the man to his outfit. "I don't want yellow-bellied bastards like him hiding their lousy cowardice around here," Patton shouted. A medical examination revealed, however, that the soldier was also suffering from malaria and high fever, and that seemed to end the matter.

Three days later, Troina was taken, but the Germans were still fiercely contesting Patton's advance on Messina. Then, on August 10, Patton visited another field hospital and there was a repetition of the first incident. Seeing a man who was shaking convulsively, Patton asked, "What happened to you?"

"It's my nerves," the soldier sobbed. "I can't stand the shelling any more."

Patton again lost control of himself. "Your nerves, hell," he shouted. "You're just a goddammed coward."

The soldier cried and Patton struck him. "Shut up," he said. "I won't have these brave men who have been shot see a yellow bastard crying." Patton struck him again and then shouted, "You're going back to the front lines. You may get shot and killed, but you're going back to fight. If you don't, I'll stand you up against a wall and have a firing squad shoot you on purpose." This time, Patton's outburst created a furor. Within a week, it was common gossip among the U.S. troops on the island.

On the morning of August 17, elements of the Seventh Army led by General Lucian Truscott entered Messina and took possession of the Town Hall. They were just minutes ahead of a breathless British officer who had raced in to claim it for Monty. At 10:30, Patton entered

A U.S. tank speeds through a town in Sicily on way to Palermo.

the city in triumph, wearing on his chest his second Distinguished Service Cross. It had been awarded to him the day before by General Eisenhower. Patton then issued an order congratulating his men on their victory. It said, in part:

"Soldiers of the Seventh Army:

"Born at sea, baptized in blood, and crowned with victory, in the course of thirty-eight days of incessant battle and unceasing labor, you have added a glorious chapter to the history of war.

"Pitted against the best the Germans and Italians could offer, you have been unfailingly successful. The rapidity of your dash, which culminated in the capture of Palermo, was equalled by the dogged tenacity with which you stormed Troina and captured Messina. . . . You have destroyed the prestige of the enemy. . . . Your fame shall never die."

Patton's elation was not to last long. On the same morning that Patton had entered Messina as a conquering

74

Ike and Patton were all smiles when this picture was taken in 1943, but later Ike severely rebuked him for slapping U.S. soldiers.

hero, Eisenhower received a report at his headquarters in Algiers of the second soldier-slapping incident. It had been written by the commanding officer of the hospital involved and sent through channels. When the report was confirmed, Ike wrote Patton a blistering letter in his own hand. He told Patton that his behavior had been "despicable," and ordered him to apologize to "the soldiers he had insulted," the hospital personnel present, and finally to representatives of each of his divisions.

Patton complied immediately, although the humiliation was enormous, and also wrote a letter of apology to Eisenhower. In it he said:

"I am at a loss to find words to express my chagrin and grief at having given you, a man to whom I owe everything, and for whom I would gladly lay down my life, cause for displeasure with me.

"I assure you that I had no intention of being either harsh or cruel in my treatment of the two soldiers in question. My sole purpose was to try and restore in them a just appreciation of their obligation as men and soldiers."

To the representatives of his divisions, Patton sounded almost humble. This is what he told them:

"In my dealings with you, I have been guilty on too many occasions, perhaps, of criticisms and loud talking. I am sorry for this and wish to assure you that when I criticize and censure, I am wholly impersonal. For every man I have criticized in this Army, I have probably stopped, talked to, and complimented a thousand. . . . You know that I have never asked any of you to go where I have feared to tread. I have been criticized for this, but there are many General Pattons and there is only one Seventh Army. I can be expended, but the Seventh Army must and will be victorious. I am very proud of you. . . . You are magnificent fighting men. Your deeds in Sicily will fill the pages of history for a thousand years."

So far, newspaper correspondents had kept the slapping story "under their hats" by mutual agreement. Ike asked them to continue to do so. To a group of assembled press representatives Ike said:

"Patton's emotional tenseness and his impulsiveness are the very qualities that make him, in open situations, such a remarkable leader of an army. In pursuit and exploitation there is need for a commander who sees nothing but the necessity of getting ahead. The more he drives his men, the more he will save their lives. . . . Patton is such a commander. I feel, therefore, that Patton should be saved for the great battles facing us in Europe."

Ike was satisfied to rebuke Patton, rather than relieve him of his command. It seemed then that the matter would soon be forgotten. Unfortunately for Patton, a radio commentator in the United States who did not feel bound by the gentlemen's agreement abroad heard about the slapping incidents and broadcast the story in November. The broadcast created an uproar at home, and there were demands everywhere for Patton's dismissal. One American Legion post in Iowa said, "These are American soldiers and not Germans. If our boys are to be mistreated, let's import Hitler and do it up right."

Neither Marshall nor Eisenhower would yield to the pressures to relieve Patton of his command, but more and more the command was becoming a sinecure. In Italy, the U.S. Fifth Army, made up in part of elements of the U.S. Seventh, was in action against the enemy, but General Mark Clark, not Patton, was commanding it. Though he bore it manfully, Patton was in disgrace and he knew it. The glory of the conquest of Sicily was gone. So, too, was the pleasure of beating Montgomery into Messina. In his book, A Soldier's Story, General Bradley sums up Patton's experience in Sicily in this fashion:

"In that unhappy part of his career, George's theatrics brought him much contempt, and his impetuousness outraged his commanders.

"Canny a showman though George was, he failed to grasp the psychology of the combat soldier. . . . George irritated them by flaunting the pageantry of his command. He traveled in an entourage of command cars followed by a string of nattily uniformed staff officers. His own vehicle was gaily decked with oversized stars and the insignia of his command. These exhibitions did not awe the troops as perhaps Patton believed. Instead, they offended the men as they trudged through the clouds of dust left in the wake of that procession. In Sicily, Patton, the man, bore little resemblance to Patton, the legend."

A U.S. tank rumbles past wrecked German vehicles after breakout in France. Patton's armored columns ripped German defense line.

CHAPTER VII: ☆ ☆ ☆ ☆
PATTON'S DASH
ACROSS FRANCE

In the fall and winter after the conquest of Sicily, when Patton was in so much disfavor, he and his staff made a tour of the Mediterranean, visiting the Holy Land, Egypt, Corsica, and Malta. As a keen student of history, Patton was stimulated by these visits, and found much to marvel at in the relics of antiquity.

The Army sponsored this tour for two reasons. By now the Germans had come to respect and fear Patton as an adversary, and were watching his movements as a clue to where the Allies would strike next. By moving Patton all around the Mediterranean, the Army hoped to keep the Germans guessing. At the same time, by promising Patton nothing definite in the way of a future command, it was letting him stew in his own juice. By the middle of January, Patton was thoroughly depressed. He was beginning to fear that he would be left to rot indefinitely in his *palazzo* on Sicily.

Then, on January 22, 1944, Patton received a message summoning him to England. Eisenhower, it seemed, had a job for Patton after all. The cross-Channel invasion of the continent, code-named "Overlord," was only months away. Ike wanted Patton to command the U.S. Third Army in that great crusade. There was a hitch in the offer, however, one that was potentially troublesome. Ike had already decided that he wanted General Omar Bradley to command the Twelfth Army Group, which would consist of the First and Third U.S. Armies. That meant that Bradley, who had been Patton's subordinate in North Africa and in Sicily, would be Patton's boss in western Europe. Eisenhower summed up his reasons for choosing Bradley as follows:

"He was a keen judge of men and their capabilities and was absolutely fair and just in his dealings with them. Added to this, he was emotionally stable and possessed a grasp of larger issues that clearly marked him for high office."

Bradley himself had misgivings about having Patton under his command, but he did not express them to Eisenhower. Perhaps Eisenhower sensed them anyway, for he assured Bradley that Patton would submit "without rancor." "All Patton wants," Ike said, "is the chance to get back into the war. For a time he thought he was through."

Patton and Monty seem the best of friends here, but both were good actors. Gen. Omar Bradley stands between the two rivals.

Ike apparently knew his man, for whatever Patton's private feelings may have been, he cheerfully accepted the assignment. He seemed bent on proving to Ike, and everyone else, that he could and would be "the good soldier."

Bradley's fears that Patton would resent the change in their status and that Patton's impetuous habits would be hard to control were soon dissipated. According to Bradley, "George soon caused me to repent these uncharitable reservations, for he not only bore me no ill will, but he trooped for Twelfth Army Group with unbounded loyalty and eagerness. . . . Before many months had passed, the *new* Patton had totally obliterated my unwarranted apprehensions; we formed as amiable and contented a team as existed in the senior command. No longer the martinet that had sometimes strutted in Sicily, George had become a judicious, reasonable, and likable commander. . . . I shall go on believing that the

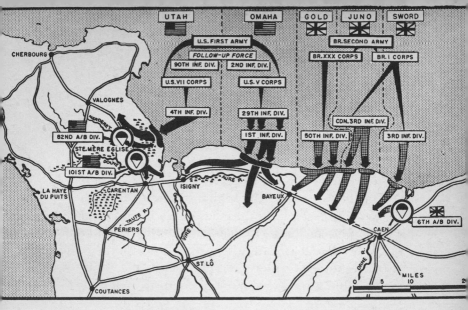

Invasion plan for France called for Allies to land on Normandy beaches, then swiftly capture Cherbourg, a major port for supplies.

private whose face he slapped in a hospital ward did more to win the war in Europe than any other private in the Army."

Though Ike had given him a new command, there were numerous indications that Patton was not completely out of the doghouse yet. For one, the Third Army, which Patton was to command, wasn't even in England yet. It was 5,000 miles away, in Texas, and only a token force would arrive before February. Also, Patton was assigned to very pleasant quarters, but they were in central England—180 miles from London, where the real planning for Overlord was taking place. Finally, the Overlord plan called for the U.S. First Army under Bradley and the British Second Army under Montgomery to invade the continent on D-Day. The Third Army would not get into the fight until at least 15 days later, and possibly much more.

Patton's view of the Overlord plan generally was that

it was too timid. The plan called for the initial establishment of a beachhead, and then for its expansion into a "lodgement" within 90 days. There, however, the plan stopped. It contained no provision for a "breakout" operation, the kind that Patton was so eager to execute.

Meanwhile, Patton was again assigned to a role of decoying the Germans. Although the invasion was scheduled to take place on the beaches of Normandy, elaborate steps were taken to give German intelligence sources the impression that Patton's army would land in the Calais area, much further east. The Germans fell for the hoax and built up a major force there to halt "*Armeegruppe* Patton." This diversion of German strength helped substantially to insure the success of the actual Allied landings in Normandy.

Although Patton had given Eisenhower assurances that he would be on his best behavior as the new Third Army commander, nevertheless he managed to stir up a teapot tempest while in England. In April, Patton was invited to speak before a "Welcome Club" that had been set up for the entertainment of Third Army troops near his headquarters at Knutsford. Patton accepted the invitation, and was assured that his remarks would not be quoted in the press. In his off-the-cuff address, Patton sought to charm his English hosts. He told them that he thought such clubs were a fine idea, and would help bring about better understanding between the United States and Britain. Then he added, "Since it is the evident destiny of the British and Americans to rule the world, the better we know each other the better the job we will do."

Everyone seemed delighted by the speech and Patton was given a vote of thanks. Unfortunately for Patton, his

Patton delivers a speech in England, shortly before the invasion of France. One such speech stirred up a "teapot tempest."

remarks *were* quoted by the press and overnight another storm developed. Patton had not mentioned the Russians as being among those destined to rule the postwar world, and many people took this as a serious affront to our wartime ally. Again a hue and cry was raised against Patton, and once again Ike was severely embarrassed. As in the slapping incident, Ike stuck by Patton, but his patience was wearing thin. In a telegram to Patton, Ike said he was retaining him as the Third Army commander "solely because of my faith in you as a battle leader and for no other motives." To Bradley, Ike said, "If I have to apologize publicly for George once more, I'm going to have to let him go, valuable as he is. I'm getting sick and tired of having to protect him."

According to Ike, "During my investigation George came to see me and in his typically generous and emo-

U.S. troops wade onto Normandy beach from landing craft, D-Day.

tional fashion offered to resign his commission so as to relieve me of my embarrassment. When I finally announced to him my determination to drop the whole matter and to retain him as the prospective commander of the Third Army, he was stirred to the point of tears. At such moments General Patton revealed a side of his makeup that was difficult for anyone except his intimate friends to understand. His remorse was very great, not only for the trouble he had caused me but, he said, for the fact that he had vehemently criticized me to his associates when he thought I might relieve him. His emotional range was very great and he lived at either one end or the other of it. I laughingly told him, 'You owe us some victories; pay off and the world will deem me a wise man.'"

Before long, Ike was preoccupied with more momentous problems. The invasion of the continent began on June 6, and by nightfall the Allied armies had managed

St. Lo, France, one day after "Cobra" saturation air bombardment.

to secure a beachhead on the Normandy coast despite some very strong German resistance. The effort to expand the beachhead into a substantial lodgment, however, was almost painfully slow. In Normandy, the farmlands were divided by hedgerows—thick, earthen ramparts topped by trees and brambles. These stout hedgerows formed a natural line of defense for the Germans, more formidable, perhaps, than any they could have devised. Tanks could not break through them but had to belly over them instead. As they did so, their unprotected undersides were exposed to savage fire from well-concealed German 88 guns. As a consequence, the Allied advance in Normandy was proceeding by yards and falling well behind the original Overlord schedule.

On July 10, more than a month after D-Day, Bradley conceived a plan to break out of the Normandy hedgerow country. He called it "Cobra." The plan called for a saturation air bombardment of an area three and a half miles wide by one and a half miles deep in the vicinity of St. Lo. Once the heavy bombers had done their job of pulverizing the enemy, infantry and armored divisions of the First Army would crash through the "carpeted" area. "Cobra" went off on July 25, and it struck a devastating blow at the enemy. By noon of the following day, a major breakthrough had been achieved by the First Army.

Patton had arrived in France on July 6 and set up his headquarters in an apple orchard high up on the Cherbourg peninsula. The Third Army, however, had not yet been activated, and Patton was already terribly restless. On July 20, he heard the news that an attempt to assassinate Hitler had been made, and he raced down to Bradley's headquarters.

"For God's sake, Brad," he pleaded, "you've got to get me into this fight before the war is over. I'm in the doghouse now and I'm apt to die there unless I pull something spectacular to get me out."

Cobra, of course, was the perfect opportunity for Bradley to use Patton. Bradley wanted to exploit the breakthrough at St. Lo to its fullest and, in his own words, "no other commander could have matched him [Patton] in reckless haste and boldness." On July 27, Bradley ordered Patton into action with the VIII Corps, an armored outfit which was scheduled to become part of the Third Army when it was activated. Patton's objective was the town of Avranches at the base of the Cherbourg peninsula. Its capture would unhinge the German line. The *breakthrough* achieved at St. Lo could then become a *breakout,* a fanning out of mobile forces behind the Germans that would shatter their entire defense line in France.

Patton's two armored divisions were soon pushing hard towards Avranches, slowed only by the wrecked and burning vehicles left by the retreating Germans along every road. Patton would tolerate no delay. Once, for example, he found the Sixth Armored Division stalled before a river. Its commanding general was studying a map to find a spot where the river might be shallow enough to cross. Patton waded into the stream himself, looked at some Germans a short distance away, and then returned. "Okay," he said to the general, "take them across. This sewer isn't more than two feet deep."

Patton's advance was so rapid that it threw the Germans into utter confusion. His armored columns were overrunning German command posts even before their occupants knew they were being attacked. Some German commanders made last-second getaways. Most were captured. Overwhelmed by Patton's armor, the Germans yielded Avranches on July 31.

The next day, the Third Army was to become operational. (Bradley would then become Twelfth Army Group Commander and General Courtney Hodges would take over command of the First Army from him.) Patton wanted to imbue his staff officers with his philosophy of combat, and he addressed them as follows:

"Now, gentlemen, doubtless from time to time there will be some complaints that we are pushing people too hard. I don't give a good goddam about such complaints. I believe in the old and sound rule that an ounce of sweat is worth a gallon of blood. The harder we push, the more Germans we'll kill, and the more Germans we kill, the fewer of our men will be killed. . . .

"There's another thing. . . . Forget this business of worrying about our flanks. We must guard our flanks, but not to the extent that we don't do anything else. . . . Flanks are something for the enemy to worry about, not us.

"Also, I don't want to get any messages saying, 'I'm holding my position.' We're not holding anything! Let the Hun do that. We are advancing constantly. . . .

"Our basic plan of operation is to keep on advancing regardless of whether we have to go over, under, or through the enemy. We have one motto: *'L'audace, l'audace, toujours l'audace!'* [Audacity, audacity, always audacity!] From here on out, we will always be audacious."

With the Third Army operational, Patton began showing what he meant by audacity. By August 4, Patton's armored columns were streaking in four different directions. One column was sweeping westward across the Brittany peninsula towards the port of Brest. Another was pushing southwest towards the port of Lorient. A third was stabbing east in the direction of Le Mans and the Seine River. And a fourth was moving north to St. Malo! This was the kind of slashing, mobile warfare that Patton had always dreamed about, and now he was jubilant. The Germans, who had introduced lightning warfare in 1939-1940, were stunned by the power and speed of Patton's advances.

At the same time, Patton was also causing the United States Army some alarm. Patton had ordered General Troy Middleton, one of his ablest subordinates, to race on towards Brest without bothering first to block the neck of the Brittany peninsula against a possible German counterattack. In doing this, Patton had countermanded Bradley's orders. Middleton was worried about being

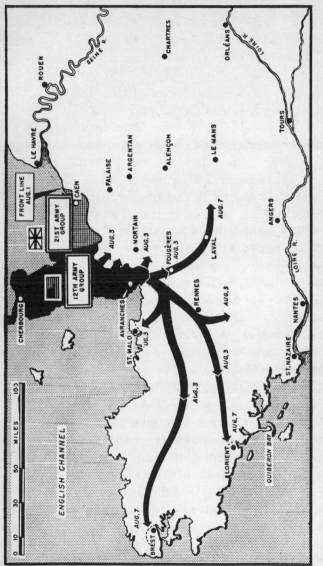

Map shows Third Army thrusting in four different directions early in August. Germans were stunned by speed of Patton's advances.

marooned on the Brittany peninsula with 80,000 men and told Bradley so on August 2. Bradley, who was a careful and methodical planner, didn't like it.

"Dammit," he said to Middleton, "George seems more interested in making headlines with the capture of Brest than in using his head on tactics."

In fact, however, there was little chance of Patton's making headlines at this time. A strict censorship had been clamped on Patton's activities since July 27 in an attempt to conceal his presence from the enemy. It was not until August 12 that Bradley asked Eisenhower to lift the veil of censorship from Patton and the Third Army. Ike turned thumbs down on the proposal. "Not yet," he said. "After all the troubles I've had with George, I have only a few gray hairs left on this poor old head of mine. Let George work a while longer for his headlines." But a few days later, Ike relented and Patton's heroics were soon big news back home. Bradley was not displeased. "George was stimulated by headlines," he said. "The blacker the headlines, the more recklessly he fought."

Meanwhile, the position of the German army in France was rapidly becoming untenable. As early as July 30, Field Marshal Gunther von Kluge, who was then the German Commander-in-Chief in the west, had sent a radio message to Hitler informing him of the hopelessness of the situation there. The message said, "As a result of the breakthrough of the enemy's armored spearhead, the whole Western front has been ripped open." Von Kluge favored an orderly retreat to the Seine to build a new defense line there. But Hitler had contrary ideas. He ordered von Kluge to regroup his battered

Seventh Army and counterattack westward to retake Avranches! This was audacity, too. For if von Kluge *could* recapture Avranches, he would not only reseal the Normandy lodgment, he would isolate Patton's rampaging forces outside it. Instead of being a tiger on the loose, Patton would be a sitting duck.

On August 7, von Kluge launched a determined attack westward employing five panzer and SS divisions as the spearhead of his drive. The attack succeeded in reaching Mortain, but then was halted by elements of the First Army. In truth, von Kluge did not have the resources for such an ambitious counterattack and knew it, but he would not disobey Hitler.

Now the German Seventh Army suddenly found itself in a potentially disastrous position. As it was pushing westward, Patton's forces were encircling it from the southeast. At the same time, Montgomery's forces were encircling it from the northeast. Patton was driving up towards the town of Argentan. Monty was headed down towards the town of Falaise. Only 12 miles separated the two towns. If the 12-mile gap could be closed, von Kluge's army would be completely surrounded and faced with certain destruction.

On the evening of August 12, Patton's XV Corps, consisting of two infantry and two armored divisions, took Argentan. Monty's drive from the north, however, was stalled, and 18 miles still separated the British and American forces. Now Patton pleaded with Bradley to let him move on to Falaise and close the gap.

"Let me go on to Falaise," he said, "and we'll drive the British back into the sea for another Dunkirk." (This was a facetious jibe at the British who, in 1940, had been

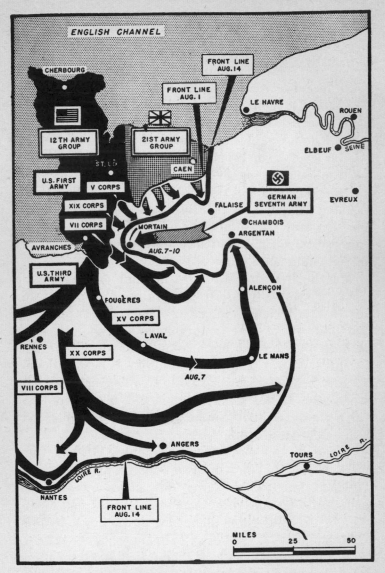

ENGLISH CHANNEL

CHERBOURG

FRONT LINE
AUG. 14

FRONT LINE
AUG. 1

LE HAVRE

ROUEN

SEINE

ELBEUF

12TH ARMY
GROUP

21ST ARMY
GROUP

ST. LÔ

CAEN

U.S. FIRST
ARMY

V CORPS

FALAISE

GERMAN
SEVENTH ARMY

EVREUX

XIX CORPS

CHAMBOIS

VII CORPS

MORTAIN

ARGENTAN

AVRANCHES

AUG. 7-10

U.S. THIRD
ARMY

ALENÇON

FOUGÈRES

XV CORPS

LAVAL

RENNES

XX CORPS

LE MANS

VIII CORPS

AUG. 7

ANGERS

TOURS

LOIRE R.

LOIRE R.

NANTES

FRONT LINE
AUG. 14

MILES
0   25   50

While the German Seventh Army pushed toward Mortain, it was nearly encircled by Patton on the south, Montgomery on the north.

driven off the continent at Dunkirk by vastly superior German forces.)

"Nothing doing," Bradley replied. "You're not to go beyond Argentan. Just stop where you are and build up on that shoulder."

Bradley gave two reasons for holding Patton at Argentan. First, he "was fearful of colliding with Montgomery's forces" if Patton had continued on to Falaise. "A head-on meeting between two converging armies . . . becomes a dangerous and uncontrollable maneuver unless each of the advancing forces is halted by a prearranged plan." Second, Bradley doubted whether the XV Corps was strong enough to hold Falaise, even if it could have taken it. The Germans were now stampeding out of the Falaise gap to escape entrapment, and Bradley feared that they "might have trampled Patton's position in the onrush."

Patton, of course, raged at being held at Argentan, and was convinced that Bradley's decision was in part political. Falaise lay well within the British sphere of operations, and it would doubtless have been very embarrassing to Montgomery, who was himself quite a prima donna, to let Patton take it. Here again Patton saw evidence of what he called "Allyism," which to him meant favoritism towards the British on the part of Eisenhower and, sometimes, Bradley.

In any event, Montgomery did not succeed in closing the Falaise gap until August 19, and in the meantime thousands of German troops were able to escape to fight again another day. Nevertheless, the Mortain counterattack had ended in a crushing defeat for the Germans. Nineteen German divisions had been chewed up in

A group of German soldiers behind white flag surrender in Paris.

the Mortain-Falaise pocket, and 70,000 of the enemy killed or captured. The remnants of von Kluge's forces were now fleeing pell-mell back towards the Seine. The liberation of Paris was only days away.

Even while Patton was waiting impatiently for Monty to close the gap at Falaise, he had sent elements of his Third Army streaking eastward towards the Seine River and Paris. By August 21, they had forced the Seine both north and south of the French capital and were in a position to take the city within days, if not hours. But Patton was not to have this plum assignment. The honor of liberating Paris from the Germans was given to General Jacques LeClerc's Free French 2nd Armored Division, which had been part of the Third Army. According to Bradley, "Any number of American divisions could more easily have spearheaded our march into Paris. But to help the French recapture their pride after four years of occupation, I chose a French force with the tricolor on

94

their Shermans." Paris was liberated by this force on August 25, with a substantial assist from the underground movement, and Patton manfully swallowed his disappointment.

The German collapse in France soon became complete. The once all-powerful German armies were now reeling back in panic to their own frontier. Their only hope now of making a stand lay in the steel and concrete fortifications of the Siegfried Line along their western frontier. Meanwhile, the Allies were strengthened by the addition of the U.S. Seventh Army and the French First Army, which had landed in southern France on August 15 and swept up to the German frontier in less than a month.

Now Ike was faced with another major problem: What was the best way to crack through the Siegfried Line? Two differing plans were offered to Ike, one by Montgomery, the other by Bradley. Montgomery's plan called for a northern thrust through Belgium to the German Ruhr, a great industrial region. This thrust would be made by Monty's two armies, the British Second and the Canadian First, and the entire U.S. First Army. Under this plan, the Third Army would take a purely defensive position along the Meuse River in eastern France while Monty raced on to Berlin. To Bradley, this looked like a repetition of Sicily, where Monty was to take Messina while Patton merely protected his flank. Bradley's plan called for a double thrust into Germany. One thrust would be made in the north through Belgium by Monty's two armies assisted by one corps of the U.S. First Army. The other thrust would be made by the Third Army and two corps of the First Army to the south through the Ger-

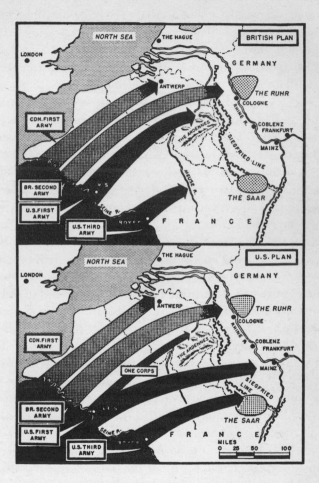

Monty's plan for invasion of Germany (top) consigned Patton to a minor role. Bradley's plan (below) gave Patton a major role.

man Saar, a coal-mining area. In Bradley's plan, Patton would have a predominant role.

While Ike was trying to decide between the two plans, another problem was beginning to plague him. Following the St. Lo breakout, the Allied armies advanced so swiftly across France that, towards the end of August, supplies could not keep up with them. Most supplies were still being landed at Cherbourg, the only major port the Allies possessed, and the Normandy beaches. These were now, in some instances, more than 300 miles behind the rampaging Allied armies. French railroads were almost useless because of devastating Allied air attacks both before and after D-Day. The job of transporting the enormous quantities of gasoline, ammunition, and other equipment needed by the Allied armies fell to Army supply trucks. Despite the most heroic efforts of the truck drivers, it was impossible for them to overcome the problems of distance, time, and need. (The Third Army alone required 6,000 tons a day of gas, oil, and ammunition to keep it going.) Before long, it was evident that a rationing of supplies would have to begin.

On August 23, Eisenhower indicated that he favored Monty's plan for a single thrust into Germany through Belgium. That meant that a priority in supplies would have to be given to Monty's two armies and the U.S. First Army. The Third Army was not to stand still, but was to advance *as far as its supplies would permit it.* Actually, Patton's supply situation was becoming more desperate each day. At first Patton saw his supplies choked off when a large number of his trucks were diverted to the First Army's use. Bradley tried to help Patton by calling on C-47 air transports to airlift gasoline supplies to the Third Army. Soon, however, these planes were also diverted to Monty's drive in the north. As Patton saw his gasoline supplies dwindling day by day, he bellowed in anger and anguish. On August 30, for example, he learned that one of his top tank commanders had halted a drive towards Commercy for fear of running out of gasoline. Patton called his commander and roared over the phone, "You get off your fanny as fast as you can and move on until your engines run dry, and then move forward on foot, goddammit!" That same day, Patton requisitioned 400,000 gallons of gasoline for his Army. The next day, he got 31,000 gallons.

Patton was now beside himself. He was only 35 miles from Metz, in eastern France, and 70 miles from the Saar, with almost nothing to bar his way into Germany except the still empty fortifications of the Siegfried Line. He was sure that, given the gasoline he needed, he could crash through and end the war that fall.

On August 31, Patton pleaded with Bradley. "Dammit, Brad," he said, "just give me 400,000 gallons of gasoline and I'll put you inside Germany in two days."

Bradley was sympathetic. "But," he wrote, "400,000 gallons of gasoline? George might as well have asked for the moon."

The cut-off of supplies to Patton by the Allied high command raises some pointed questions. Was it done in a deliberate effort to curb Patton's rashness? Patton certainly thought this was the case. In his memoirs, entitled *War As I Knew It*, he concludes with this statement:

"Practically throughout the campaign, I was under wraps from the Higher Command. This may have been a good thing, as perhaps I am too impetuous. However, I do not believe I was, and feel that if I had been permitted to go all-out, the war would have ended sooner and more lives would have been saved. Particularly I think this statement applies to the time when, in the early days of September, we were halted owing to the desire, or necessity, on the part of General Eisenhower in backing Montgomery's move to the north. At that time there was no question or doubt but that we could have gone through and on across the Rhine within ten days. This would have saved a great many thousand men."

Could Patton have gone across the Rhine and, presumably, on to Berlin to end the war at that time? No one in the Allied High Command believed it then, nor do the survivors believe it now. An aide to General Bradley recently said:

"Suppose we had given Patton 400,000 gallons of gasoline. What assurance did we have that, without close air support and only very limited air supply, he could have driven 600 miles to Berlin? And even if he had been able to get into Berlin, what chance would he have had of holding it? A good panzer task force manned by Hitler Youth would have chopped him off from the rear."

By August 31, the Third Army had run out of gasoline. Its tanks needed spare parts, and its soldiers needed shoes, socks, and heavy underwear. There was nothing for Patton to do but call a halt. He was reduced to making a few short feints just to keep the enemy guessing.

Patton buttons up against the cold while touring Third Army front.

CHAPTER VIII: ☆☆☆☆
PATTON ON THE
DEFENSIVE

The Third Army's drive in August 1944, had carried it farther and faster than any army in history. By August 26, it had advanced 400 miles eastward, inflicted more than 70,000 casualties on the enemy, and captured 65,000 more. Field Marshal Erwin Rommel wrote that, although the Americans had distinguished themselves in Tunisia, "we had to wait until the Patton Army in France to see the most astonishing achievements in mobile warfare." Josef Stalin, the Russian dictator, remarked, "The Red Army could not even have conceived, never mind have executed, the Third Army's incredible dash across France."

Now, on August 31, Patton found himself halted, not by German resistance, but by a shortage of gasoline.

Patton was, however, a resourceful as well as a determined man, and he soon managed, by one means or another, to scrounge enough gasoline to get his Army moving again. Patton called his favorite technique of getting gasoline the "rock soup method." He described it this way:

"A tramp once went to a house and asked for some boiling water to make rock soup. The lady was interested and gave him the water, in which he placed two polished white stones. He then asked if he might have some potatoes and carrots to put in the soup to flavor it a little, and finally ended up with some meat. In other words, in order to attack, we had first to pretend to reconnoiter, then reinforce the reconnaissance, and finally put on an attack—all depending on what gasoline and ammunition we could secure."

There were other techniques of obtaining gasoline. The Third Army had captured enormous quantities of excellent wines and liqueurs from the enemy. Any C-47 pilot who airlifted a load of gasoline to the Third Army could be sure of not going back empty-handed. There was still another method, which Patton commented on:

"There was a rumor, which, officially, I hoped was not true, that some of our Ordnance people passed themselves off as members of the First Army and secured quite a bit of gasoline from one of the dumps of that unit. . . . This is not war, but it is magnificent."

By such methods, Patton rolled stubbornly ahead. In theory, his scant gasoline rations should have halted him along the Meuse River line. But Patton managed to drive 30 miles beyond it to the Moselle River and established a bridgehead across that waterway south of the city of Metz. By this time, however, German resistance was beginning to stiffen all along the western

High German officers inspect antitank gun behind Siegfried Line.

front. A new German commander, Field Marshal Walther Model, a hero of the Russian front, was stemming the panic in the German armies and reorganizing them once again into effective fighting forces. In spite of the increasing resistance, Patton succeeded in breaching the Moselle along a 50-mile front, but by then he was at the end of his supply line. On September 25, Bradley ordered Patton to "hold present position until supply situation permits resumption of offensive." In short, Patton was to sit down along the Moselle and take the defensive.

Meanwhile, the thrust to the German frontier by Monty's two armies and the U.S. First Army in the north was experiencing serious difficulties. By the end of September, the Allies were stalled all along the Siegfried Line by a combination of the gasoline drought and sharply increased German opposition. The period of "breakout" had ended, and with it the Allies' hopes of an early German surrender.

The six weeks that followed Bradley's order on Sep-

GIs struggle to free a jeep stuck in mud caused by heavy rains.

tember 25 to take the defensive along the Moselle River were a period of great frustration for Patton. In his memoirs, Patton wrote, "For the first time in our experience we were not advancing rapidly, if at all. We were fighting, with inadequate means, against equal or superior forces in excellent defensive positions, and the weather was against us."

Almost everything during this period seemed to go against Patton. The weather *was* awful. It rained constantly during October and November, turning the battlefield into a great quagmire. Thousands of soldiers came down with trenchfoot, a crippling condition caused by exposure of the feet to wetness and cold. At one point, in fact, trenchfoot was disabling as many Third Army men as enemy fire. The supply situation continued to be bad, and now artillery shells, as well as gasoline, had to be severely rationed. In addition, the Germans were reinforcing their line with hastily organized units of fresh, though largely inexperienced, troops.

Despite all these discouraging elements, Patton was

103

not a man to remain passive for long, if he could help it. On September 27, he began an assault on Metz, a city that was guarded by extremely heavy fortifications. The biggest fort defending the city, Driant, was a particularly formidable obstacle. Situated atop a hill, it consisted of a central fort plus three huge concrete blockhouses and three large bunkers. All of them were enclosed by dense barbed wire, concrete machine gun nests, and moats. A preliminary attack on this fort on September 27 hardly dented it at all. A second attack on October 3 did not fare much better. This time, some GI's managed to penetrate the central fort, but the Germans kept coming up from their underground tunnels and inflicted heavy casualties on the American platoons from the rear. Finally the attackers were forced to withdraw.

Patton was angry and insisted, "I cannot allow an attack by this army to fail!" But on October 11, Patton, conceding that he could not capture Fort Driant at that time because "the ammunition supply was extremely precarious," called off the assault. Despite this setback, the Third Army continued to expand its bridgeheads across the Moselle, in anticipation of a renewed offensive, and to patrol aggressively.

Patton did not have to wait long to renew his attack. On October 18, Ike decided to resume the offensive in November, rather than wait until the following spring when the supply situation would be much better. Once again Monty argued in favor of a single thrust to the Rhine north of Cologne, which would have consigned Patton to a defensive position along the Moselle, possibly for the remainder of the war. Bradley again argued for a much broader thrust. Under his plan, Monty's forces would attack to the Rhine River north of Cologne; the U.S. First Army and the new U.S. Ninth Army would attack towards Cologne; to the south, Patton's Third Army would break through the Saar to the Rhine River in the vicinity of Frankfurt. In this attack, supplies would be shared more or less equally by all the armies involved. This time, Ike chose Bradley's plan and the attack was set to begin on or after November 5.

Patton was set to jump off for the Saar on the 5th, but it rained all that day and all of the next two days. Without air support, Patton chose to postpone his attack. Finally Patton decided that, with or without air support, his attack would begin on November 8. On the afternoon of November 7, Generals Manton Eddy and Robert Grow pleaded with Patton to postpone the jump-off date. Not only was it still raining hard, but the Moselle River had reached a flood crest, the highest in 50 years, and had washed out almost all the bridges across it. In his memoirs Patton wrote that he then asked them "whom they wished to name as their successors, because the attack was to go off as scheduled. They immediately assented and, as usual, did great work."

Early on the morning of November 8, a heavy artillery barrage from more than 700 guns preceded the Third Army's attack. Then Patton's army of 220,000 men began crossing the Moselle on rafts and flimsy assault craft, an operation that would take five days to complete. At 7:45 A.M. Bradley called Patton to see if he was attacking. He seemed delighted when Patton told him the Third Army was moving ahead. Then Eisenhower got on the line and said, "Georgie, I expect a lot of you. Carry the ball all the way."

The going, however, proved to be slow, tedious, and costly. The trenchfoot problem was acute at this time, and now Patton was faced with a serious shortage of infantry replacements, as well as ammunition. (This was true of other U.S. Armies as well. It was due largely to the diversion of too many men to the Pacific.) In some cases, his rifle companies were at little more than half strength, and Patton had to pull men out of clerical and other noncombat units to augment them. Despite rain, floods, washed-out bridges, and shortages, Patton was gradually pushing the enemy back and encircling Metz, the fortress city that had repelled his frontal assault in October. About November 19, according to Patton, "the last German column to attempt to get out of Metz was caught on the road by a company of medium tanks from the Sixth Armored Division, who opened fire on them at a range of about 150 yards. I visited the road and have seldom viewed a scene of greater devastation."

By the 22nd, the resistance within Metz had crumbled, and Patton's men were shelling the remaining forts with German guns and ammunition. Three days later, Patton entered the city in triumph, reviewed his victorious troops, and dispensed medals and profane compliments with equal relish.

A U.S. patrol in Metz seeks out German snipers in buildings.

Now Patton pushed on to the Saar River, and on the evening of December 2 crossed it at Saarlautern. He was inside Germany for the first time, with a toehold in the Siegfried Line. The breakthrough was to be accomplished, as at St. Lo, by means of a devastating preliminary air bombardment. For three days, starting December 19, 1,000 heavy bombers were to pulverize the Siegfried Line in the vicinity of Kaiserslautern. Patton called it "probably the most ambitious air blitz ever conceived." Patton's forces now began pressing towards the breakthrough area for their date with the Air Force.

Meanwhile, the weather was so bad that Patton decided to call for Divine intervention. On or about December 14, Patton summoned Col. James H. O'Neill, Chaplain of the Third Army, to his headquarters and directed him to pray for fair weather. The conversation, according to Col. Paul D. Harkins, Patton's deputy Chief of Staff, went as follows:

Gen. Patton: "Chaplain, I want you to publish a prayer for good weather. I'm sick and tired of these soldiers having to fight mud and floods as well as Germans. See if we can't get God to work on our side."

Chaplain O'Neill: "Sir, it's going to take a pretty thick rug for that kind of praying."

Gen. Patton: "I don't care if it takes the flying carpet. I want the praying done."

Chaplain O'Neill: "Yes, sir. May I say, General, that it isn't a customary thing among men of my profession to pray for clear weather to kill fellow men?"

Gen. Patton: Chaplain, are you teaching me theology or are you the Chaplain of the Third Army? I want a prayer."

Chaplain O'Neill: "Yes, sir."

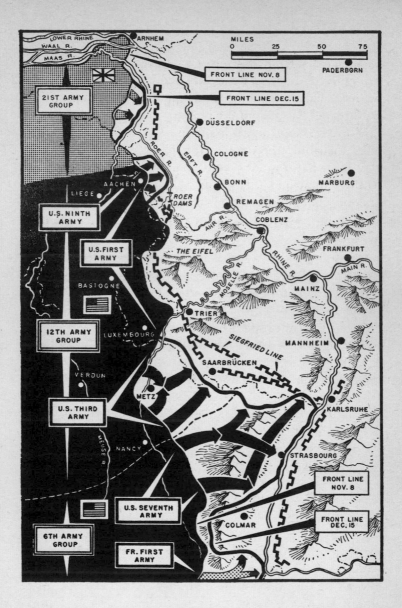

After encircling Metz, Patton's Third Army broke through to the Saar and gained a toehold in the Siegfried Line.

Chaplain O'Neill did write a prayer calling upon the Almighty "to restrain these immoderate rains with which we have had to contend [and] grant us fair weather for Battle. . . ." Patton had the prayer printed on a Christmas card to be issued to all his men. By the time the cards were distributed, however, the Third Army was a long way from its original destination of Kaiserslautern. For while Patton and other U.S. Army commanders were planning to crack the Siegfried Line and bring Germany to its knees, Adolf Hitler was secretly hatching a plan of his own.

On the night of December 16, Patton received a call from Bradley's headquarters ordering him to transfer his 10th Armored Division to Troy Middleton's VIII Corps, now part of the First Army, that same night. Patton roared in anger. He was planning to use the 10th Armored for his big breakthrough at Kaiserslautern. This would jeopardize his scheme. Finally Patton got Bradley on the phone. According to Patton, "I protested very strongly, saying that we had paid a high price for that sector [Saarlautern] so far, and that to move the 10th Armored to the north would be playing into the hands of the Germans. General Bradley admitted my logic, but said that the situation was such that it could not be discussed over the telephone."

The truth was, the Germans had opened an all-out attack that day in the Ardennes area with four armies and were running roughshod over the VIII Corps' four divisions. At Allied headquarters, there was consternation over the suddenness and severity of the German attack. Before very long, Patton would have to shift almost his entire Army up to the Ardennes. In so doing, he would make military history again.

Germans struck furiously in Ardennes. hoping to turn tide of war.

CHAPTER IX:
THE BATTLE OF THE BULGE

The German counteroffensive in the Ardennes, which came to be known as "The Battle of the Bulge," caught the Allies completely unawares. Some evidence of a German buildup had been observed by Allied intelligence officers, particularly in the area of Cologne. Yet it was almost uniformly believed that these forces were poised for nothing more serious than a limited "spoiler" attack along the Roer River, north of the Ardennes, to blunt the Allied offensive. The Allies, in fact, were quite sure that by now the Germans were beaten and no longer capable of launching a major offensive.

Yet, with the utmost secrecy, Hitler had succeeded in assembling a very substantial force with which he now hoped to deal the Allies a severe blow. Two of the four armies were panzers—the Sixth SS Panzer Army under General "Sepp" Dietrich, and the Fifth Panzer Army commanded by General Hasso von Manteuffel. The German master plan, drawn by Field Marshal von Runstedt, called for these two armies, with some 600 tanks, to slash through the Ardennes to Antwerp, Belgium, while the other two armies protected their flanks. If the Germans *had* reached Antwerp, they would have split the Allied armies in two, inflicting on them a setback of major proportions.

Why had the Germans chosen to launch a panzer attack through the Ardennes, a wooded area with very few roads? It was, they knew, the most thinly defended section of the American line. There were not enough U.S. troops to launch a winter offensive *and* to secure every inch of the line. In a calculated risk, only four divisions were assigned to hold an 88-mile front in the Ardennes that had been quiet for a long time. Those four divisions belonged to Gen. Troy Middleton's VIII Corps.

The German drive began with all the old blitzkrieg fury at 5 A.M., December 16. "We gamble everything now," von Runstedt told his troops. "We cannot fail." Within two days, the force of the attack, aided by the element of surprise, had crushed the center of the U.S. line in the Ardennes. Yet even now, while Middleton's front was crumbling, there were hopeful signs. On the north, the main German thrust by the Sixth SS Panzer Army had been blocked at Malmedy by Hodges' First Army. At nearby St. Vith, U.S. forces were fighting a grim holding action, upsetting the Germans' timetable. On the south, the U.S. shoulder was also holding. In the center of the bulge that the Germans had pushed out,

111

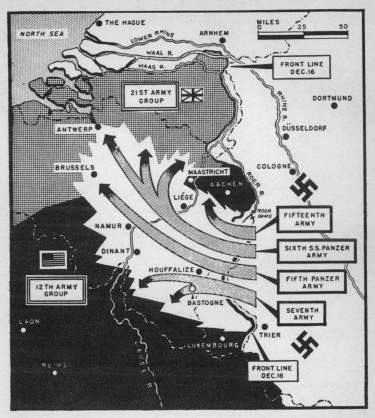

German plan called for a lighting drive through the Ardennes to Antwerp, which would have cut the Allied forces in two.

von Manteuffel's panzers were now racing towards the town of Bastogne, a vital road junction. Bradley immediately ordered Middleton to hold Bastogne "at all costs." Elements of the 10th Armored, released by Patton, raced north to reinforce tanks of the 9th Armored already dug in there. And that evening, after a wild ride, the 101st Airborne roared into town in trucks to reinforce its defenders.

By now Bradley had begun to evolve a strategy of defense against the German attack. While Hodges' First Army grappled with the Germans on the northern and center rim of the bulge, Patton's Third Army would slash into it from the south. That day, Bradley told Patton that he would have to call off his offensive in the Saar and wheel his army up north to the Bulge. At first, Patton was dismayed at having to give up his own offensive, but finally he accepted it with a shrug. "What the hell," he said, "we'll still be killing Krauts."

On the following day, December 19, there was an historic meeting at Verdun at which Eisenhower addressed his top commanders. "The present situation is to be regarded as one of opportunity for us and not of disaster," Ike said. "There will be only cheerful faces at this conference table." According to Ike, Patton then quipped, "Hell, let's have the guts to let the − − go all the way to Paris. Then we'll really cut 'em off and chew 'em up." Everyone smiled at that, including Patton.

Then Bradley asked Patton how soon he could get the Third Army into action at the Bulge, about 90 miles north of his present position. Almost any other commander would have estimated at least 98 hours, and then held his breath. Patton, however, said he could have three divisions in action against the Germans by the morning of December 22. Ike thought Patton was being facetious and told him so. But Patton replied that he had already set the wheels in motion and meant what he said.

The job of shifting an army of more than 225,000 men and all its equipment to a new front 90 miles away within a few days would have been extremely difficult under even the best circumstances. Some 133,000 vehicles of all kinds—trucks, half-tracks, tanks, and jeeps—would

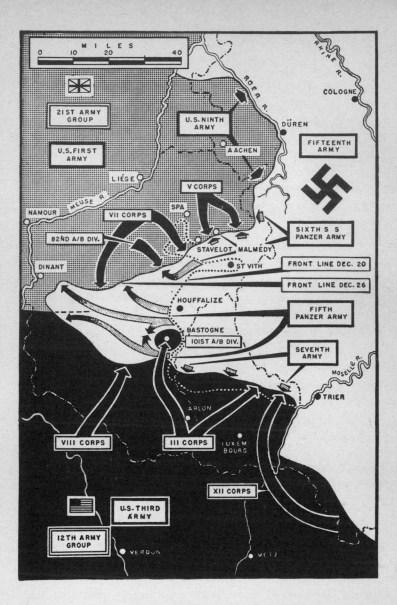

By December 26, the Germans were halted everywhere in the "bulge," and Patton's armor relieved U.S. troops in Bastogne.

have to travel around the clock, bumper to bumper, to accomplish it. About 20,000 miles of new telephone lines would have to be strung, and 62,000 tons of supplies shifted to new depots and dumps. But the circumstances were far from helpful. All this now had to be done in the midst of a winter blizzard, with temperatures near zero, and over ice-covered roads.

Somehow, almost miraculously, Patton and his staff got the job done. Disregarding standard blackout regulations, Patton told his men to drive with all headlights blazing at night and with throttles wide open so as not to lose a minute. By midnight, December 19, Patton's troops were already moving northward. From the windows of his office in Luxembourg, Bradley could see the steady procession of the men and vehicles of the Third Army. In canvas-topped trucks, troops wearing heavy overcoats still caked with the mud of the Saar huddled against the icy cold. Tank commanders standing in the turrets of their vehicles had wrapped woolen scarves around their faces to protect them from frostbite. Day and night these columns rattled northward. By December 22, advance elements of the Third Army were fighting the Germans in the Bulge. "The speed with which the Third Army turned its forces north," Bradley wrote, "astonished even those of us who had gambled in the Ardennes on the mobility of our army."

Meanwhile the situation at Bastogne had become critical. At first, von Manteuffel's panzers had bypassed the town in their westward drive. Then, as the Germans became increasingly aware of the town's strategic importance, they had encircled it. On December 22, they demanded that General Anthony C. McAuliffe, com-

Third Army infantrymen fire on Germans in advance to Bastogne.

mander of the 18,000 defenders at Bastogne, surrender his garrison. McAuliffe answered them in a word: "Nuts!" As Patton sped north, his main objective became to relieve the beleaguered American force at Bastogne.

Patton's orders to his staff were, as usual, direct and uncompromising. "I want every man to be fighting," he said. "There are to be no reserves. Everybody fights. Everyone in this Army must understand that we are not fighting this battle in any half-cocked manner. It's either root hog, or die. Shoot the works!"

On December 22, the men of the Third Army received Patton's Christmas card containing Chaplain O'Neill's prayer for good weather. The following morning, the skies were bright and clear for the first time since the Battle of the Bulge had begun. Now the Air Force would be able to fly missions in support of the ground troops. Patton was jubilant. "That O'Neill sure did some potent praying," he told a subordinate. "Get him up here. I

116

Relief of the Bastogne garrison is celebrated with a handshake.

want to pin a medal on him." When O'Neill reported, Patton said, "Chaplain, you're the most popular man in this headquarters. You sure stand in good with the Lord and soldiers." Then he formally presented O'Neill with the Bronze Star.

With assistance from the Air Force, Patton pushed his Fourth Armored Division towards Bastogne. Despite violent German counterattacks, which Patton called "rather discouraging" on December 24, the Fourth Armored managed to grind out gains. Patton visited all the trouble spots, shouting, cursing, and praising his men on. By Christmas Eve, only six miles separated the Fourth Armored from the encircled garrison at Bastogne. In his diary the next day, Patton wrote: "Christmas dawned clear and cold. Lovely weather for killing Germans, although the thought seemed somewhat at variance with the spirit of the day."

Christmas passed without any letup in the fighting. Then, on December 26, elements of the Fourth Armored rolled into Bastogne and made contact with the defenders. The corridor the tanks opened into Bastogne was still too narrow and dangerous, however, to permit other vehicles to enter. But by the 27th it had been widened sufficiently to let through supply trucks and ambulances to evacuate the wounded. The siege of Bastogne had been broken.

On the same day that the Fourth Armored moved into Bastogne, the German attack in the Bulge was brought to a standstill éverywhere. Although there would still be some extremely hard fighting in the days ahead—the Germans tried desperately to cut Patton's corridor into Bastogne—the period of greatest danger was over. The German offensive in the Bulge was now doomed. On the 29th, the Germans began pulling back, and soon a feeling of cautious optimism ran through the U.S. forces. At midnight on New Year's Eve, Patton noted in his diary, "All guns in the Third Army fired rapid fire for twenty minutes on the Germans as a New Year's greeting. When the firing ceased, our forward observers stated they could hear the Germans screaming in the woods."

On New Year's Day, Patton congratulated his Third Army on "the speed and brilliancy of achievements . . . unsurpassed in military history." After wishing his men continued victories "to the end that tyranny and vice shall be eliminated, our dead comrades avenged, and peace restored to a war-weary world," Patton concluded with the words of the U.S. victor in the Mexican War, General Winfield Scott:

"Brave rifles, veterans, you have been baptized in fire and blood and have come out steel."

Capture of this bridge intact over Rhine at Remagen influenced Ike's decision to launch "double thrust" drive into Germany.

CHAPTER X:
TO THE RHINE AND BEYOND

By the end of January, the German bulge had been completely hammered out. The Allies were now pressing against the Siegfried Line along its entire length, poised to deliver the death blow to Nazi Germany. As for the Germans, their defeat in the Ardennes had been nothing less than a disaster. To mount the offensive, Hitler had scraped the bottom of the German manpower barrel. Boys of 16 and middle-aged men had been drafted into special *Volksgrenadier* divisions to provide the German army with reserves. Not only had the Ardennes offensive failed to accomplish its objectives, but it had cost the Germans more than 250,000 casualties and hundreds of tanks and guns. (U.S. casualties were 59,000.) While the Germans were exhausting their carefully husbanded resources in the Bulge, the Russians opened up a great offensive in the east and, on January 19, captured Warsaw, Poland. The understrength German armies were beginning to collapse, but in the west, at least, they still had the advantage of the Siegfried Line.

Once again the Allies in the west were faced with the dilemma of how to break through to the heart of Germany. As usual, Montgomery pressed for an offensive by his armies north of Cologne. This time, he wanted the U.S. Ninth Army to support his attack *under his command.* The U.S. First Army would play a supporting role, but Patton's Third Army was again relegated to a purely defensive position. Monty's plan was approved by Eisenhower, and Patton was ordered to hold.

Patton was outraged. In his memoirs he wrote, "I told

Concrete "dragon's teeth," part of the Siegfried Line, were meant to stop tanks. Patton found them no great obstacle.

him [Bradley] I was the oldest leader in age and combat experience in the United States Army in Europe, and that if I had to go on the defensive, I would ask to be relieved. He stated that I owed too much to the troops and would have to stay on. I replied that a great deal was owed to me and, unless I could continue attacking, I would have to be relieved."

Bradley still favored the "double thrust" into Germany, and he, too, wanted to use the Third Army in an aggressive role. But SHAEF (Supreme Headquarters, Allied Expeditionary Force) had issued written orders assigning Patton to the defensive. What was Bradley to do? Here, it appears, he entered into a little conspiracy to help Patton. According to Bradley, "Now, with Eisenhower's consent, I ordered Patton to mount an offensive. . . . It was to be strong enough to keep the enemy from shifting his strength . . . but not strong enough to arouse the objections of Monty."

Patton's limited offensive was to pierce the enemy's Siegfried Line in a mountainous area called the Eiffel. It lies just north of the Saar, where Patton's army was after the Battle of the Bulge. There he was to secure a bridgehead across the Kyll River in preparation for a full-scale drive to the Rhine. But, Bradley wrote, "this latter phase was not to begin until Monty was safely anchored on the Rhine opposite the Ruhr."

Patton, however, was not easily contented with what he called "an aggressive defense." No sooner had he pushed his army into the Eiffel, than he began to cast his eyes on the city of Trier, which was not included in the original plan for his offensive. First Patton coaxed SHAEF into letting him borrow the 10th Armored Division, which he needed for the operation, for a short time. (The 10th Armored was then being held in reserve by

SHAEF.) When Patton failed to take Trier within the allotted time, SHAEF demanded the return of the 10th Armored. Now Patton carried his little conspiracy with Bradley a bit further. In his memoirs, Patton wrote, "I called Bradley at dark as I had promised, to tell him that I was not yet in Trier, but was within eight kilometers of it, and asked if I could keep on. He said to keep on until he was ordered by higher authority to stop me, and added that he would keep away from the telephone."

On March 1, Trier fell to the 10th Armored and elements of another division. The next day Patton received a message from SHAEF ordering him to bypass Trier "as it would need four divisions to capture the city." Patton immediately wired back, "Have taken Trier with two divisions. What do you want me to do—give it back?"

In his diary Patton noted, "The lesson to be gained from this is that successful generals make plans to fit circumstances, but do not try to create circumstances to fit plans."

As for the Siegfried Line defenses that he had penetrated, Patton was not at all impressed. He wrote, "Pacifists would do well to study the Siegfried and Maginot Lines, remembering that these defenses were forced. . . . In war the only sure defense is offense, and the efficiency of offense depends on the warlike souls of those conducting it."

On March 5, Bradley signalled Patton to jump off from his positions across the Kyll and head for the Rhine, which Monty called "the greatest water obstacle in western Europe." On the following day, Patton sent his 4th Armored Division under General Hugh Gaffey streaking towards the Rhine in the vicinity of Coblenz. Within two

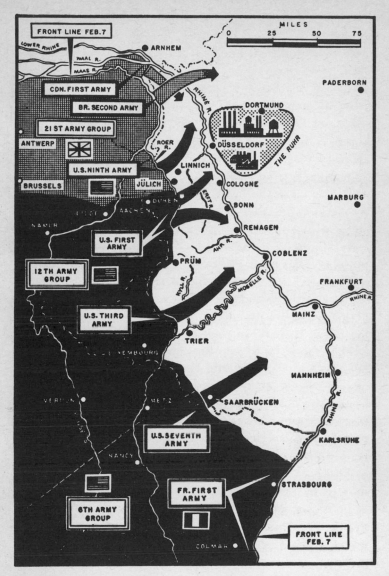

The Allied drive to the Rhine was launched on a broad front, and German resistance began to crumble.

days, the 4th Armored had driven 35 miles towards its objective, in a salient no wider than the road it travelled. Bradley called this "the boldest and most insolent blitz of the western war."

Enemy resistance west of the Rhine was now crumbling all along the front. As U.S. tanks rolled through the streets of German villages, the people shuttered their homes and hung out white sheets. The once mighty German war machine was dissolving, and large numbers of demoralized troops were starting to surrender to the Allies. As far as they were concerned, the German cause was *kaput* (finished). Only the most fanatic Nazis still had any illusions about staving off defeat.

By March 12, Patton's army was poised all along the Moselle River from Trier on the west to Coblenz on the east, where the Moselle flows into the Rhine. To the south was the Saar, the German industrial region that Patton had been preparing to invade when the Battle of the Bulge diverted his forces. Now Patton got the green light to move south into the Saar. At the same time, the U.S. Seventh Army, under the overall command of General Jacob Devers, was ordered to move into the Saar from the Third Army's former positions facing the Siegfried Line. Patton regarded the Saar as his plum, and told Bradley as much. "Tell Devers to get out of the way," he said, "or we'll pick him up with the Krauts."

Within 24 hours, the Third Army was swarming down into the Saar in a slashing, almost reckless advance. Once again the 4th Armored led the way, penetrating deep into the Saar and into the Seventh Army's zone as well. As Patton's charging armored columns rapidly cut off the enemy's escape route to the Rhine, the Germans panicked. Their retreat soon became a disorderly rout in which senior German commanders lost touch with their troops. One day, for example, a German corps commander drove into a field of dispirited German soldiers and asked them why they were not out fighting the Americans. A moment later, a U.S. military policeman clapped a hand on his shoulder and invited him to join the other prisoners of war. Within eight days, Patton had mopped up the Saar and taken more than 60,000 prisoners.

As for the prisoners of war, they were more fortunate than some German soldiers in the Saar. In his memoirs, Patton describes coming upon "one of the greatest scenes of destruction I have ever contemplated. A German column entering the road from the northwest, and consisting mainly of animal transport and guns, was struck on the right flank by a company of medium tanks of the 10th Armored Division. The Germans were moving up a rather steep canyon with a precipitous cliff on their left, while the tanks came in between them and the mountain. For

One of many German tanks knocked out in advance to Rhine.

more than two miles horses and vehicles were pushed over the cliff. You could see the marks of the tank treads on the flanks and shoulders of the horses, and see the powder marks on the men and horses where they had been shot at point-blank range. In spite of my pride in the achievement of the 10th Armored, I was sorry for the poor creatures."

By March 22, eight divisions of the Third Army were on the west bank of the Rhine below Coblenz, set for the kill. And now Patton was finally free to plunge into the heart of Germany, for, shortly after March 15, Eisenhower decided to discard Monty's "single thrust" invasion strategy in favor of Bradley's "double thrust" strategy. That meant that the Third Army would now be a full partner in the invasion of Germany, rather than a kind of poor relation. While Monty's armies and the U.S. Ninth Army encircled the heart of Germany from the north, the U.S. First and Third Armies would encircle it from the south. Patton could go now as fast as his armored columns and German resistance would permit him.

Now that he was no longer required to "hold" while Monty carried the ball, Patton once again sought to outdo his old rival. The First Army had already obtained a bridgehead across the Rhine at Remagen, but Monty hadn't crossed it yet, though he was making very elaborate preparations to do so. Prime Minister Winston Churchill had personally journeyed to the Rhine to witness Monty's epic crossing. In his memoirs, Churchill set the scene: "Eighty thousand men, the advance guard of armies a million strong, were to be hurled forward. Masses of boats and pontoons lay ready. On the far side stood the Germans, entrenched and organized in all the strength of modern fire-power."

Meanwhile Patton was touring his front on the Rhine and coming to the conclusion that there, at least, the Germans were thoroughly demoralized and near collapse. On the morning of March 23, Bradley received a telephone call from Patton.

"Brad," Patton said, "don't tell anyone but I'm across." "Well I'll be . . ." Bradley replied. "You mean across the Rhine?"

"Sure am," Patton said. "I sneaked a division over last night [March 22]. But there are so few Krauts around there they don't know it yet. So don't make any announcement—we'll keep it a secret until we see how it goes."

Without the benefit of any prior artillery or aerial bombardment, Patton's 5th Infantry Division had ferried across the Rhine on rafts and in assault boats, suffering only 34 casualties. On the evening of the 23rd, Patton telephoned Bradley again. "Brad," he shouted at the top of his voice, "for God's sake tell the world we're across. We knocked down 33 Krauts today when they came over our pontoon bridges. I want the world to know the Third Army made it before Monty starts across."

Monty, in fact, had started across on the afternoon of March 23, and before long *all* the Allied armies were sweeping across Germany from the west. Except for the desperate delaying tactics of diehard Nazis and SS troops, enemy opposition faded. Meanwhile, Russian armies were invading Germany from the east, and the days of Hitler's Third Reich were clearly numbered.

Ike, Bradley, Patton (right) view burned bodies of Nazi death-camp victims. Patton likened it to "a cannibalistic barbecue."

As Patton's Third Army raced across Germany, it came upon the first of several Nazi concentration camps where millions of Jews and other prisoners were put to death under the most degrading circumstances. Patton was so revolted by the sight that he called Bradley and insisted that he and Eisenhower see it for themselves. "You'll never believe how bastardly these Krauts can be," he said, "until you've seen this pest hole yourself."

In his memoirs, Patton described the death camp at Ohrdruf as "the most appalling sight imaginable." Referring to the burned bodies of the camps' victims, Patton said, "One could not help but think of some gigantic cannibalistic barbecue."

Here's how Bradley described the scene when he and Eisenhower visited it with Patton:

"The smell of death overwhelmed us even before we passed through the stockade. More than 3,200 naked, emaciated bodies had been flung into shallow graves. ... Lice crawled over the yellowed skin of their sharp, bony frames. A guard showed us how the blood had congealed in coarse, black scabs where the starving prisoners had torn out the entrails of the dead for food. Eisenhower's face whitened into a mask. Patton walked over to a corner and sickened. I was too revolted to speak. For here death had been so fouled by degradation that it both stunned and numbed us."

Patton insisted that the mayor of the town and his wife view the camp. "On going home," Patton reported, "these two committed suicide."

Patton was no less tender towards the feelings of a captured SS general. This general was not a combat officer, but a Nazi political official who had been governor of the French province of Lorraine. He had committed and condoned numerous atrocities against French civilians. Patton questioned the man personally. This is how the conversation went, according to Patton's nephew, Fred Ayer, Jr.:

Patton (who was dressed in heavy field boots): "I always wear boots like these when I'm anywhere around you SS Nazis. You will stand at attention when I speak to you and you will preface every answer to me with 'Sir.' I have captured a number of German generals, but you are the most sordid son of a bitch of them all. You aren't a soldier. You're a goddammed party official. Our records show that you committed some very grave offenses in Lorraine."

SS official: "Sir, I did nothing I am ashamed of. I may have made some mistakes, but only those of human judgment."

Patton: "What do you mean, human judgment? Are you

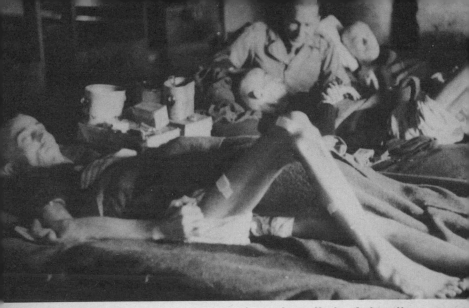

Liberated American prisoners of war show effects of starvation.

talking about Nazi judgment, or the judgment of decent people? What about the hostages you shot?"

SS official: "Sir, there were times when that was absolutely necessary for the protection of the Reich."

Patton: "The war crimes commission will decide that."

Then, to a guard, Patton said, "Take the dirty bastard away and throw him in the deepest cell we have."

On March 26, four days after the Third Army had slipped across the Rhine, Patton made what he himself called his only error of the entire campaign in Europe. About 50 miles behind the German lines, in the town of Hammelburg, was a *stalag* (prison camp) in which many captured GI's were being held. One of the prisoners was Patton's own son-in-law, a fact that Patton said he was not aware of at this time. On the evening of the 26th, Patton dispatched a small task force consisting of about 293 men and 50 vehicles, including tanks, to liberate the American prisoners at Hammelburg. The task force was commanded by Captain Abraham Baum, a husky tanker from the Bronx, New York.

It was, unfortunately, much too small to undertake such a daring mission. Soon after the task force set out, it ran into a gauntlet of enemy fire. On the 28th, when Baum's tanks crashed through the prison stockade, it had only one third of its original strength. While the jubilant POW's took off into the hills, Baum started his small force back to his own lines. It was soon pounced upon by German Tiger tanks determined to destroy the raiders. On the morning of the 29th, Baum was out of gas and ammunition, and wounded. He and the few other survivors of his mission surrendered.

Patton brooded about the incident for some time, but Bradley did not rebuke him for it. "While I deplored the impetuousness that had prompted Patton," Bradley wrote, "... failure itself was George's own worst reprimand."

U.S. and Russian soldiers meet on Elbe River bridge at Torgau.

Though some pockets of enemy resistance still had to be forced, in April the war became little more than a cakewalk. While American divisions marched into the interior of Germany, German POW's marched backward along the same roads to prison camps. On April 25, a patrol from Hodges' First Army made contact with a Russian army group at Torgau on the Elbe River, a prearranged meeting point. The end of the war was only two weeks away.

On April 22, Patton's Third Army began the last phase of its campaign in Europe. For some time, there had been a widespread rumor that diehard Nazis had stored away a huge amount of war materials in the Austrian Alps, where they were preparing to make a last-ditch stand. This rumored Alpine fortress was called the "National Redoubt." Actually, the Redoubt existed only in the imagination of a few fanatic Nazis, but the Allies had no way of knowing that and the rumor had to be checked out. From Bavaria in southeast Germany, Patton began a drive towards the Austrian frontier and then plunged down the Danube towards Linz, almost half way to Vienna. Meeting little resistance, Patton finally buried the myth of an enemy Redoubt in Austria. Meanwhile, other elements of the Third Army were pressed up against the Czech border, and Patton was pleading for permission to cross it.

"Why," Bradley asked Patton, "does everyone in the Third Army want to liberate the Czechs?"

Patton grinned and replied, "On to Czechoslovakia and fraternization! How can you stop an army with a battle cry like that?" (U.S. soldiers had been forbidden to mingle with German women, a policy called non-fraternization.) On May 4, Patton got permission to cross the Czech border, but was not allowed to go beyond Pilsen. Patton objected to being halted there, insisting that he could easily go on to Prague, the Czech capital. However, Prague, like Berlin, had already been earmarked for liberation by the Russians, and Patton was required to hold at Pilsen. Patton later said that he was very much "chagrined" at not being allowed to go on to Prague and, "if the Russians didn't like it, let them go to hell."

On May 8, Patton issued his final casualty report of the war for the Third Army and the enemy it had met. It was as follows:

Third Army

Killed	21,441
Wounded	99,224
Missing	16,200
Nonbattle casualties	111,562
Total	248,427

Enemy

Killed	144,500
Wounded	386,200
Prisoners of war	956,000
Total	1,486,700

On May 9, 1945, the surrender of Germany became official. The day was called VE Day, for Victory in Europe. Col. Paul D. Harkins, who edited Patton's memoirs, summed up the Third Army's record this way: "It had gone farther, captured more prisoners, crossed more rivers, liberated more friendly territory, and captured more enemy territory than any army ever before in American history." On VE Day, Patton, who was now a four-star general, issued a victory order to his soldiers, concluding:

"During the course of this war I have received promotions and decorations far above and beyond my original merit. You won them: I as your representative wear them. The one honor which is mine and mine alone is that of having commanded such an incomparable group of Americans, the record of whose fortitude, audacity, and valor will endure as long as history lasts."

In June, Patton returned home for the last time, and received the almost frenzied homage of the people of Boston. Standing in the lead car of a motorcade, Patton looked to his niece, Anne Ayer, "like Alexander the Great, Caesar, and Napoleon all rolled into one, returning from their wars." No doubt, Patton must have impressed many others in that cheering multitude the same way.

Back home for victory parade, Patton was met by his wife and son.

Eisenhower, Patton, President Harry S.Truman stand at attention as U.S. flag is raised in Berlin at end of the war in Europe.

CHAPTER XI: ☆☆☆
AFTER THE WAR

In times of peace, Patton was a bored, restless, pent-up man, and the end of the war in Europe was bound to leave him feeling depressed. Even before the war ended, he was worried about it. In a letter to his wife dated April 12, 1945, Patton said in part:

"I love war and responsibility and excitement. Peace is going to be hell on me. I will probably be a great nuisance."

In August, Patton indicated his unhappiness with peacetime existence in a diary entry:

"Another war has ended, and with it my usefulness to

the world. It is for me personally a very sad thought. Now all that is left to do is to sit around and wait the arrival of the undertaker and posthumous immortality."

Peace had come to Europe in May 1945, but in the Pacific the war was still being fought furiously against Japan. Patton had expected that he and the Third Army would soon be taking on the Japanese, but in this he was mistaken. Instead of being sent to the Pacific, he was appointed military governor of the province of Bavaria, Germany. Unfortunately, it was not a role for which Patton was well-suited by temperament or experience, and before very long he found himself in trouble again.

The immediate objective of the wartime allies—the United States, Britain, France, and Russia—following VE Day was to "de-Nazify" Germany. That meant removing all Nazi officials from positions of importance in the country and otherwise ridding it of the Nazi influence. In Bavaria, however, Patton was quite evidently lagging in carrying out the de-Nazification program. Former Nazis still held key positions in government there. Twice Eisenhower warned Patton against "mollycoddling" Nazis and to carry out the de-Nazification program as he had been ordered.

Had Patton, the man who had sickened at the sight of a Nazi death camp, and who had constantly blasted Nazis as "Huns" and much worse, now changed his mind about them? Patton insisted that he still hated Nazis as much as anyone. He defended the use of Nazis in office, however, on the grounds of expediency—they were needed to keep vital public services running, at least for the time being. But beyond that, Patton had another reason for not cracking down on former Nazi officials. He was already advocating a war with Soviet Russia, and in such a

Patton genially shakes hands with a Russian general after VE Day.

war he thought the Germans would be useful allies, whether or not they had been active Nazis. "I don't think we ought to mistreat people whom we will need so badly," he told Col. Harkins.

Patton had been thinking about a war with Soviet Russia even before the war against Germany had ended. Stories of Soviet oppression related to him by eastern European refugees aroused his sympathies, and his earliest meetings with Russian officers seemed to provoke an almost violent antipathy towards them. "Russian officers," he wrote in his diary, "with few exceptions give the appearance of recently civilized Mongolian bandits." In a letter home, he wrote, "We have destroyed what could have been a good race [the Germans] and we are about to replace them with the Mongolian savages and all Europe with communism." Before long, Patton was calling for a war with Russia in which the Germans would serve as allies.

On one occasion, Patton expressed such sentiments to General Joseph T. McNarney, Eisenhower's chief deputy in Europe. McNarney had telephoned to tell Patton that the Russians were complaining that he, Patton, was too slow in disarming and disbanding several German army units in Bavaria. The telephone conversation was later related by Col. Harkins to General Harry H. Semmes, author of the biography, *Portrait of Patton*. It was as follows:

Patton: "Why do you care what those Russians think? We are going to have to fight them sooner or later, within the next generation I am sure, maybe a whole lot sooner. Why not do it now while our army is intact and the damn Russians can have their hind end kicked back into Russia in three months? We can do it easily with the help of the German troops we have, if we just arm them and take them with us. They hate the bastards."

McNarney: "Shut up, Georgie you fool, this line may be tapped and you will be starting a war with those Russians with your talking!"

Patton: "I would like to get it started some way; that is the best thing we can do now. You don't have to get mixed up in it at all if you are so damn soft about it and scared of your rank—just let me handle it down here. In ten days, I can have enough incidents happen to have us at war with the sons-of-bitches and make it look like their fault. So much so that we will be completely justified in attacking them and running them out."

Thoroughly shocked, McNarney hung up. This conversation, and similar statements made by Patton, ultimately brought about Patton's downfall. They were contrary to American policy at the time, which was to seek cooperation with Russia in the postwar world. They were also at variance with public opinion, which, after so many years of war, wanted to "bring the boys back home." And the notion of using German troops shocked everyone to whom Patton mentioned it.

Patton was ordered to shut up, but this was something he could not do easily. "Few generals could surpass Patton as a field commander," Bradley wrote, "but he had one enemy that he could not vanquish, and that was his own quick tongue." On September 22, Patton held a press conference at which he belittled the de-Nazification program and said that the military government "would get better results if it employed more former members of the Nazi party in administrative jobs and as skilled workmen." Then Patton made a statement that sealed his doom:

"This Nazi thing—it's just like a Democratic-Republican election fight. . . . The 'outs' are always coming around saying that the 'ins' are Nazis. . . . More than half the German people were Nazis and you'd be in a hell of a fix if you tried to remember all the Party members."

This statement, in which Patton implied that Nazis weren't much different from Democrats or Republicans, was published widely in newspapers throughout the United States. It provoked a storm of protest, and once again Patton was the center of a scandal.

Eisenhower, who on two previous occasions had stood by Patton when he might have dropped him, showed forbearance even now. He did not relieve Patton of his command, but instead ordered him to hold another press conference and retract his statements made on the 22nd. He also required Patton to read a statement by him,

Eisenhower, on de-Nazification.

Patton called another press conference at which he read Eisenhower's statement. It said in part:

"Reduced to its fundamentals, the United States entered this war as a foe of Nazism; victory is not complete until we have eliminated from positions of responsibility and, in appropriate cases, properly punished every active adherent of the Nazi party."

Patton also apologized for the "unfortunate" comparison he had made between the Nazis and U.S. political parties, but otherwise he did not seem very penitent. He defended his policies in Bavaria and concluded by saying that "to the best of my knowledge and belief, there are no out-and-out Nazis in positions of importance whose removal has not already been carried out."

This last statement was apparently too much for Eisenhower. On September 28, he summoned Patton to his office and, after a two-hour confrontation, relieved Patton of his Third Army command. Until he died, Patton remained embittered by what he considered Ike's "ingratitude."

To soften the blow, Patton was given command of the "United States Fifteenth Army." In reality, it was not an army at all, but a small group of officers who were compiling from official records a history of the war in Europe. Patton devoted himself to writing his memoirs, which were later published under the title, *War As I Knew It*.

Patton had often said that "the only way for a soldier to die is by the last bullet in the last battle." Having survived the war, he felt that his existence now was not merely an anticlimax, but was perhaps even a little un-manly. On his last visit home in June, he told his family that he expected to die quite soon. Patton's daughter, Ruth Ellen, described the occasion:

"It was the night before Daddy was to go back to Germany. His exact words were, 'I am never going to see you again. I know this. I am going to be buried in foreign soil.'

"One of us said, 'Oh Daddy, don't be silly. The war's over now.' He said, 'Yes, I know. But my luck has all run out now. . . . I've spent it all. I have not been a good enough man in my life to be killed by a bullet like General Bee at Manassas. I don't know how it's going to happen, but I'm going to die over there.'"

Patton's words were remarkably prophetic. On December 9, 1945, he and General "Hap" Gay were riding in the back seat of a car near Mannheim, Germany. They were on their way to a pheasant hunt. Suddenly, an Army truck coming in the opposite direction swerved in front of the car to make a left turn. There was a collision which appeared, at first, to be minor. But soon it was apparent that Patton had suffered a broken neck, the result of having been thrown forward against the front seat. He was almost completely paralyzed. No one else in the accident was more than shaken up.

For 12 days Patton fought for his life in an Army hospital. At first, his condition seemed to improve. There was even talk of flying him home to a hospital in Boston. But later, complications developed and Patton began to fail. Near the end he said, "This is a hell of a way for a soldier to die." At 5:50 P.M., December 21, 1945, Patton died in his sleep of acute heart failure.

141

Patton had always said that he wanted to be buried in whatever country he fell. "That's where any soldier would want to be; and it will remind people forever of who it was that fought to set them free."

In accordance with his wishes, Patton was buried in a military cemetery in Luxembourg, the tiny country through which his Third Army had passed on the way north to Bastogne. There he joined 6,000 other heroes of the Third Army. In death, Patton would be eternally near the battlefield, among the soldiers of his command.

Many words were written in praise of Patton when he died. Perhaps the most eloquent were these from an editorial in *The New York Times:*

"History has reached out and embraced General George Patton. His place is secure. He will be ranked in the forefront of America's great military leaders. . . .

"Long before the war ended, Patton was a legend. Spectacular, swaggering, pistol-packing, deeply religious, and violently profane, easily moved to anger because he was first of all a fighting man, easily moved to tears because underneath all his mannered irascibility he had a kind heart, he was a strange combination of fire and ice. Hot in battles and ruthless, too, he was icy in his inflexibility of purpose. He was no mere hell-for-leather tank commander but a profound and thoughtful military student.

"He has been compared with Jeb Stuart, Nathan Bedford Forrest, and Phil Sheridan, but he fought his battles in a bigger field than any of them. He was not a man of peace. Perhaps he would have preferred to die at the height of his fame, when his men, whom he loved, were following him with devotion. His nation will accord his memory a full measure of that devotion."

**The flag-draped body of Gen. Patton is borne to a military ceme-
tery in Luxembourg, not far from scene of his triumph at Bastogne.**

BIBLIOGRAPHY

Army Times, editors of. *Warrior: the Story of General George S. Patton*. New York: G. P. Putnam's Sons, 1967.

Ayer, Fred Jr. *Before the Colors Fade: Portrait of a Soldier, George S. Patton, Jr*. Boston: Houghton Mifflin Co., 1964.

Bradley, Gen. Omar N. *A Soldier's Story*. New York: Holt, Rinehart & Winston, 1951.

Eisenhower, Gen. Dwight D. *Crusade in Europe*. New York: Doubleday & Co., 1948.

Farago, Ladislav. *Patton: Ordeal and Triumph*. New York: Astor-Honor, 1964.

Gavin, Gen. James M. "Two Fighting Generals: Patton and MacArthur," *Atlantic Monthly* (February, 1965).

Patton, Gen. George S. Jr. *War As I Knew It*. Boston: Houghton Mifflin Co., 1947.

Semmes, Harry H. *Portrait of Patton*. New York: Paperback Library, 1955.

Consultant: Chester B. Hansen, Lt. Col. U.S. Army ret.